40 Ways
to
Ditch the Negative
Self-Talk
That's Dragging
You
Down

Sh*t I Say to Myself

to Myself

Katie Krimer, LCSW

New Harbinger Publi

Publisher's Note

This publication is designed to provide accurate and authoritative information in regard to the subject matter covered. It is sold with the understanding that the publisher is not engaged in rendering psychological, financial, legal, or other professional services. If expert assistance or counseling is needed, the services of a competent professional should be sought.

NEW HARBINGER PUBLICATIONS is a registered trademark of New Harbinger Publications, Inc.

New Harbinger Publications is an employee-owned company.

Copyright © 2022 by Katie Krimer
New Harbinger Publications, Inc.
5674 Shattuck Avenue
Oakland, CA 94609
www.newharbinger.com

Cover design by Sara Christian; Illustrations by the author: Interior design by Amy Shoup and Michele Waters-Kermes; Acquired by Jess O'Brien

Library of Congress Cataloging-in-Publication Data

Printed in the United States of America

24   23   22

10   9   8   7   6   5   4   3   2   1   First Printing

"Sh*t just got real! Katie Krimer expertly cuts through the BS with authentically practical strategies to tame the inner assh*le living in all of our heads."

—**Jodie Eckleberry-Hunt, PhD, ABPP,** author of *Move on Motherf*cker* and *Getting to Good Riddance*

"One occupational hazard of being a psychotherapist is to rely too heavily on the question of 'Why?' Katie Krimer points out how our thoughts, among the most ephemeral of all phenomena, have a disproportionate gravitational pull on our experience of ourselves in the world. She offers alternative and practical suggestions to chip away at these persistent, limiting, and destructive thoughts, mercifully delivered in an easy-to-swallow manner. (I just wish I knew what sh*t meant…)."

—**Paul R. Fulton, EdD,** director of the certificate program in mindfulness and psychotherapy at the Institute for Meditation and Psychotherapy, part-time faculty in the department of psychiatry at Harvard University, and coeditor of *Mindfulness and Psychotherapy*

"Negative self-talk can be a really f*ing hard habit to break. Luckily for all of us, Katie Krimer's book, *Sh*t I Say to Myself,* does an amazing job of laying out super-common, unhelpful thoughts and walking us through the best ways to respond and reframe them. I want her to be my therapist! Instead, I'll settle for the next best thing: this sharp, funny, sassy, practical book."

—**Kelsey Torgerson Dunn, MSW, LCSW,** adolescent anxiety specialist, founder of Compassionate Counseling St. Louis, and author of *When Anxiety Makes You Angry*

"As a coach to high performers on the stage, screen, NFL, and MLB, I am no stranger to the ways in which we talk to ourselves impacts our well-being and success. This book is a glowing resource for helping all of us deal with that not-so-little voice in our heads. Not only does it lay out clear, proven strategies for adaptive self-talk, it also entertains with compelling stories and funny yet pithy artwork! Whether you are working on a specific goal or simply working to find more happiness and peace in a stressful world, this book is for you!"

> —**Jonathan Fader,** motivational interviewing trainer part
> of the Motivational Interviewing Network of Trainers
> (MINT), coauthor of *Coaching Athletes to Be Their Best,*
> and author of *Life as Sport*

"Katie Krimer would be the first to say that she didn't 'invent' many of the ideas in her book, but might have to follow some of her own principles to admit what will be obvious to any reader: She is a wonderful writer with a lucid style and the ability to synthesize numerous concepts to make eradicating negative self-talk an approachable, practical, enjoyable, nuanced, and non-corny enterprise!"

> —**Michael Dulchin, MD,** assistant clinical professor of
> psychiatry at New York University Langone Medical
> Center, and cofounder of both Union Square Practice and
> Sportstrata

"This book uses irreverence, wisdom, and behavioral science to help you break patterns of negative self-talk and take back your life!"

> —**Dennis Tirch, PhD,** author of *The Compassionate-Mind
> Guide to Overcoming Anxiety,* and founder and director of
> The Center for Compassion Focused Therapy

CONTENTS

It isn't the things that happen to us in our lives that cause us to suffer, it's how we relate to the things that happen to us that causes us to suffer.

—Pema Chödrön

• • •

How can we drop negativity, as you suggest? By dropping it. How do you drop a piece of hot coal that you are holding in your hand? How do you drop some heavy and useless baggage that you are carrying? By recognizing that you don't want to suffer the pain or carry the burden anymore and then letting go of it.

—Eckhart Tolle

No More Talking Shit

The part of the therapist gig that really sucks is hearing people's shitty self-talk. Over the last eight years, I've seen it come in many forms. There are the overt statements of self-hatred and there are the covert, backhanded ways of knocking ourselves down.

There are far more pleasant and effective ways to relate to your life, struggles, and busy mind. Lucky for you, if the shit you say to yourself is holding you back, I have a solution—*just don't fucking do it*. Simple. If you are ready to quit cold turkey, find your receipt and return the book, no hard feelings. Otherwise, I suggest you make yourself comfortable—changing habits of the mind is fucking *hard*.

You might be pleased to know, however, that you will be learning from a *true* expert—a recovered negative thinker and self-talker. I'm also a former insomniac, lifelong worrier and overthinker, recurring panic attack survivor, skilled ruminator, and recuperating perfectionist. (The rest of the list will be covered in the sequel, *Shit Your Therapist Went Through*).

At twenty-three, within just one week, I moved in with and then broke up with the person I thought I would marry. I didn't cope well—too fucking prideful to ask for help. This was all while pursuing my graduate degree in clinical psychology and battling some gnarly mental health diagnoses. The disillusion had hit hard—the rom-com stories I had placed on pedestals dissolved before me.

A friend handed me my first book about mindfulness called *When Things Fall Apart: Heart Advice for Hard times* by Pema Chödrön. It changed my life, namely by making me confront how damaging my inner voice had become and introducing ways to dismantle my inner fearmonger and hater.

I began making conscious changes to the language I used to talk to myself, and I dove into mindfulness practice to be more present and less judgmental of…everything. With every moment of self-compassion when life got difficult, my self-talk evolved into a much kinder version. I learned how to catch myself in negative narratives and to have more healthy conversations with myself.

Throughout these pages, we will discover different approaches to treating our minds as we would a loving friend, instead of a warring enemy. Together, we'll explore creative ways to transform self-judgment and negative thinking into self-kindness, mindful awareness, equanimity, and positivity.

As you journey through this book, consider keeping a journal or notebook (or make notes on your phone!) to complete the exercises. Take your time and respond to questions fully, reflect honestly on your experience.

So, before this book gets a home on a dusty shelf filled with unread pop-psych books, grab your notebook and kindly answer the following questions:

Has talking shit to or about yourself been effective?

Has devaluing yourself resulted in the positive, long-lasting changes you've always longed for?

Has your self-shaming skyrocketed your motivation and confidence?

Has your unkind, internal peanut gallery given you the input to make your dreams come true?

Has your approach to obstacles in your life made your life easier or more fulfilling?

If you wrote down variations of "Nope...not exactly," you're in the right place. As a therapist and mindset coach, I work with clients whose devaluing inner voice, limiting beliefs, and thought spirals affect nearly every lived experience they have. I observe how much their shitty inner voice dampens their experience of the wonders of life.

I'll say to you now what I say to my clients: You have to decide, today, that your way of thinking and the way you talk to yourself isn't working anymore. You must acknowledge the harm you're doing to your sense of self and take accountability for the choices in language that you make.

Once you confront the ways your old narratives have dragged you down, every moment in life will become an opportunity to consciously choose healthy, kind, and realistic ways to talk with yourself. Here's a disclaimer: it is impossible for us to cover every approach to negative thinking out there. No book can tell you exactly what to do. Mine certainly won't. But what matters most is that you recognize that suffering will endure if you don't change your habits of mind and that you commit to exploring and implementing any wisdom that can set you free. I hope this book will make one thing clear for you: change your inner voice or continue to suffer. It's up to you.

NEGATIVE SELF-TALK IN A NUTSHELL

You've earned a spot in my mini-workshop entitled: Nuances of Shit-Talking Yourself. Let's cover the basics first. Our brain produces thoughts, which are created by neurons firing off in pathways like an electrical circuit. Thoughts can have a positive, negative, or neutral valence, and they are typically directed at the self, others,

and the world. Types of thoughts include worries, assumptions, impressions, concepts, ideas, perceptions, questions, opinions, beliefs, narratives, and many more. Self-talk is the speech or thoughts we direct at ourselves, akin to an internal monologue, *sans* the talents of Shakespeare. Self-talk is also a conscious behavior that we use in response to certain thoughts or experiences, falling on a broad spectrum ranging from self-defeating criticism to affirming self-kindness. Whether occurring reflexively or used more consciously, *negative* self-talk damages our sense of self, our self-worth, and our self-esteem over time.

Evolution created a brain that prioritizes survival over introspection. The oldest parts of our brains were formed for self-protection, and they didn't evolve to accurately respond to the complex nature of emotional or ego threat. If our ancestors weren't sure if the rustling in the woods was a danger to their tribe, they didn't spend much time self-analyzing. The mind's fight-or-flight reflex protected them by initiating an optimal response to the potential threat.

Our brains are wired with a *negativity bias*, the hardwiring that makes certain that negative events rule our inner worlds over positive ones. Long ago, those who responded more effectively to threats went on to procreate, reinforcing how our brains functioned.

Let's also briefly touch on *egocentrism*—our tendency to be at the center of our own universe and an inability to see from the perspective of others—as it plays a role in every version of negative self-talk. I empathize for a living, and I *still* often erroneously assume that people see the world the way I do.

Cognitive biases are errors in our thinking that influence how we construct our individual realities. I want to really drive this home: our subjective reality is built from our *perceptions* of experience rather than on objective facts. Therefore, what we believe to be true about ourselves and others—not necessarily what *is* true—is what ends up determining our decisions, our judgments of self and others, and the rest of our behavior.

Our brain recognizes negative stimuli more readily and makes certain that we dwell on these negative stimuli, too. The more we pay attention to the negative, the more our mind exaggerates its importance, perpetuating the cycle of negative thinking. Our mind is not as reliable as we think, often giving us inaccurate information, which causes us to distort reality.

Cognitive distortions are negatively biased and irrational thoughts that fuel and reinforce our negative emotions and self-talk. Strengthened over time, this flawed way of thinking serves as a rubric for the harmful, diminishing language we use. Here are common categories of harmful self-talk:

Seemingly grounded

I'm not good at drawing—there's no sense in making art.

I'm afraid of heights—there's no point going to a theme park.

I hurt her, so I probably deserve to feel guilty for a long time.

Seemingly realistic

I've been on this dating app for weeks and I've only gotten asked out once. No one is into me.

I've failed two math exams—there's no way I'll be able to pass the class.

Fear or esteem based

I'll definitely get turned down by them.

This won't go well; I'm not doing it.

I should be sure to stay quiet in the conversation because I'm not that interesting.

Overtly demeaning and mean

I'm not lovable.

I'm an idiot. I'm a failure.

I'll never amount to much.

CONSEQUENCES OF NEGATIVE THINKING

We talk to ourselves in unkind, critical ways, and yet are brutally disappointed when nothing changes. We weave tall tales, perpetuating narratives about our identities and abilities, without questioning their truth or basis in reality. We convince ourselves that we're never going to get what we want in life because there is something fundamentally wrong with us. We waste precious time believing we aren't good enough and doubting ourselves, either stuck in the past or living out self-fulfilling prophecies of the future. We allow our defensive inner voice to erode communication and create conflict in our relationships. Our mind continues to let us down, and yet we continue to engage with it in all the same ways.

Imagine if every time you came to a therapist or loved one for support, they berated you, doubted you, told you all the ways you would fail, convinced you that you weren't good enough, invalidated your feelings, and minimized your suffering.

Would you wish to maintain such a relationship? It is no different when it comes to you and your mind. If the conversation you have with yourself negatively affects your self-esteem and self-worth, limits your capacity to make positive, lasting changes in your life, makes you live in fear, and regularly keeps you from experiencing tranquility and joy, it's time to fucking change it!

1. "I can't change"

Oh boy, do I love to get off to an optimistic start!

Neither reading stacks of self-help books nor going to therapy automatically means that we consistently and sincerely believe that we can change in ways that would result in epic self-growth. This brand of self-talk—"I can't change"—is covert, sneaking into the tone and language we use to put ourselves down. It keeps us from fully committing to the daily practices that lead to healthier thinking habits. Particularly for those who have gnarly self-talk, a pervasive defeatist attitude accompanies self-doubt.

To most of us, it's obvious that *anyone else* is capable of change, but having lived with ourselves for however long, we're certain that we're inept. We often fear that if we start to make moves toward change, we will find out that we are incapable of accomplishing what we set out to do. Too paralyzed by fear to act, we then confirm our original belief about ourselves—"I can't form good habits. I always stop short of making a routine." Guilt and shame often follow, which neatly close the loop, ensuring more negative self-talk and self-fulfilling prophecies.

Unfortunately, most of us aren't (yet) skilled in self-compassion practice, the magic that can soothe the pain of taking responsibility for how we've played a large role in enabling our minds to fuck us over.

If you were to express to me that nothing is changing in your life, despite going to therapy or, say, absorbing the epic wisdom in this book, I would ask how you've gone about putting into practice what you've learned. I promise that you wouldn't be the first to struggle with follow-through despite "getting it" and knowing what you "should do." Inevitably, this leaves you stagnant and consequently self-critical of your stuckness or your perceived inability to change like everyone else apparently can.

Are you notorious for the resigned, sigh-filled, "I know, I know," in response to yet another explanation of what it will take to feel better about yourself? And then say, "It's just really hard," or "I don't know how," or slip an "I can't" into the exchange?

As a fellow human who has experienced the immense challenge of battling my inner critic, I feel for you. As the sassy author of this book, however, I'll say, "You *do* know the why and the how" (see: pop-psych books, workbooks, therapist wisdom, common sense). Yes, it *is* really hard. And it's not that you *can't*—more accurately, it's that you're intimidated by the amount of effort it may take and afraid of not getting there in the end.

KNOW THAT YOU *WILL* CHANGE

Taking responsibility for your self-growth is a prerequisite to lasting change since no one else can do it for you. My first bit of good news for you is that just by getting older, you will naturally experience the process of change. If nothing else, remember that our noses and ears keep growing after death. You see? Even after life, there is growth.

Thankfully, our brain is pretty rad in one major way that (kind of) compensates for all the ways it makes our lives hard: it has *neuroplasticity*, an epic ability to develop new neuronal connections that can be rewired, resulting in the development of new habits (Doidge 2007), like overcoming our incessant catastrophic and negative thoughts.

Remind yourself that there are only two options: We scare ourselves out of taking steps toward self-growth and are guaranteed either to stay the same or to get worse. Or we ditch the old self-talk and encourage ourselves to be courageous and are, at the very least, guaranteed to experience some change, if not an epic transformation.

Here's the deal—if you avoid the risks of stepping outside of your comfort zone, you forfeit the right to lament or complain about any aspects of yourself or your life that you're displeased with. When you make your bed…you lie in it.

This chapter's exercise is a first step toward ditching your *fixed mindset* and developing a *growth mindset*. A fixed mindset means we believe that our abilities are impervious to improvement, no matter how much effort we put in. Those with a fixed mindset are typically more fearful of failure. A growth mindset means we have a flexible, hopeful, yet realistic way of coping with setbacks and can reframe our perspective to maintain motivation when working toward a goal. Those of us who can maintain a growth mindset tend to value learning from past experiences and prioritize self-growth and doing the work to become our best self (Dweck 2007).

DIGGING DEEPER

We can't create lasting change without building some dope self-awareness first.

Answer the following questions to reflect on your past attempts to change:

> What kind/amount of effort have you put into building new self-talk habits?

> What perceived or real barriers have prevented you from making the choices that lead to change?

> What fears have gotten in your way?

> How have you talked to yourself during the process of trying to change? How did you sound when you didn't see "enough" growth?

Commit to changing the language with which you speak to yourself by writing down your intention to do so. *Connect* this commitment to your intrinsic values—why is it important to you that you change? *Express* gratitude for a neuroplastic mind by saying aloud, "I am grateful that my brain is capable of changing." If you dare, affirm your capacity for change while looking at your reflection as an extra challenge. "Mirror, mirror on the wall, I'm done talking shit, once and for all."

2. "My mind sucks"

Minds can be bothers, yes. But talking shit *about* how you shit-talk yourself or about how you feel like shit or about how you are going *through* some shit—while impressively meta—is off-limits from now on. I don't let my clients get away with it, and you won't get any special treatment, either.

Life is difficult enough without us compounding any suffering with criticizing the way our mind is experiencing life. If you're wondering what constitutes judging your inner experience, here are some examples of what it can sound like: "I don't like that I'm still thinking about this." "I shouldn't be thinking this." "I'm weak for feeling this way." "I know this sounds crazy." "It's so stupid that I feel this upset." "I'm mad at myself for not being able to let go." "I hate feeling sad." "I don't think others have such a shitty mind."

I can promise I've heard every iteration. We are essentially judging our brain for functioning like…a brain. Which is like trying to fight gravity on Earth—pointless and exhausting.

Have you ever noticed how frequently you apologize, justify, disclaim, or feel embarrassed or ashamed when observing or sharing the content of your mind? Do you tend to give yourself a hard time instead of simply permitting yourself to be human? Do you criticize how self-critical you are?

We must first become experts at catching ourselves mid-judgment and course-correcting by normalizing our mind's activity. It's common to feel surprised and uneasy after becoming fully aware of how much we punish ourselves for simply having thoughts or feelings that we perceive as unpleasant or bad. Once we're consistently catching our inner critic in action, we can consciously change the way we respond. Then we can begin transforming the actual content.

BECOMING CURIOUS

Curiosity doesn't come naturally when your mind is busy judging. But when curiosity becomes your go-to response, you will have acquired an unmatched superpower. After years of consistent practice, my mind's default language is curiosity, while judgment has all but died out, joining its final resting place somewhere near the Latin I learned in high school. All I'm saying is…if I can do it, *you* can do it.

When our mind-made self thinks all the maddening things at once or when our body responds to a perceived emotional threat, we are always faced with a choice: allow fear to run the show, guaranteeing suffering from our judgmental ways; or become curious about any part of our inner experience by observing without judgment, as if we were scientists studying our own brain as it thinks, feels, and behaves. Scientists refrain from trying to control any part of the subject's natural behavior. In the same way, when we choose curiosity, we intentionally refrain from judging or trying to change the nature of the mind.

TURNING "UGH" INTO "HUH"

Next time you don't like what's going on in your noggin, take the opportunity to practice asking yourself questions instead of yielding to the temptation of playing jury. A simple yet transformative adjustment is to change the *tone* with which you speak to yourself. The same question can be posed either with an attitude, or with a sense of wonder.

Once you've gotten rid of the 'tude, you can ask yourself some of these tried-and-true exploratory questions:

"I wonder why I just had that thought?"

"What would happen if I just let the sadness stay here for a while?"

"What if I accepted that it will take me some time to change this narrative?"

"What if instead of calling myself crazy for thinking this way, I see it as human?"

"What can I learn from this moment or experience?"

Keep asking questions instead of bitching at the organ that keeps you alive. You're in for a blissful awakening.

3. "Everything I think must be true"

Imagine a scenario where you have the following thought: *I wasn't there for my BFF when they really needed me. I'm the shittiest friend ever.* Then you go on to agree with said thought: *Yep. Total shit. A good friend doesn't mess up like this.*

Feeling ashamed, you tell yourself that it would be better to stop answering their texts because there is no way to repair what you've done. Before you know it, you've lost a friendship—and not because you let them down, in fact, but because you decided that a flub (yes, even an epic one) determined your entire worth as a friend. Spoiler alert: soon you'll know to remind yourself that millions of people all over the world fuck up all the time, and it doesn't make them all shitty humans. What's more, millions of people have millions of thoughts, most of which are not based in observable fact, but rather in subjectivity (and, I should mention, tons of bias).

When it comes to *other* people being hard on themselves, not only do we show compassion for their plight, but we also confidently call them out on their harsh and inaccurate self-judgment. We are unwaveringly certain their thinking is flawed, bewildered that they'd cling so steadfastly to a mindset that makes them feel unworthy. Think about how often we respond, "That's not true!" when a friend reveals their mind's self-defeating content to us. Although I relish exposing their flawed logic, many clients will fight me to the death to prove that they are the exception to the rule.

THOUGHTS ARE NOT FACTS

Averaging a cool fifty to seventy thousand thoughts a day, the brain does not have the capacity to function as a fact-checker for every single one. Thoughts aren't inherently true or false; they are simply electrical signals that fire in your mind, which your mind then rapidly interprets. Because these signals are frequently dependent on our mood, precipitating events, and our perceptions of the world around us, our interpretation of a thought gives it its actual valence—and ultimately, its power over us. Many of our thoughts are opinions or perceptions that are based on years of conditioning. When we take our negative thoughts too seriously, the consequences pile up—we struggle to believe in ourselves, become paralyzed with fear, and our self-worth begins to deteriorate.

Remember that time you thought you were way behind everyone else your age in life? You were *absolutely certain* it was true. Or how about the time you became burned-out from your job because you told yourself you didn't *deserve* to take time for yourself to decompress? What about when you couldn't shake the guilt—making yourself feel progressively worse with each bit of negative self-talk—even after someone forgave you? Did you stop to question whether there were some holes in your logic?

To evaluate whether a thought is true or not, try asking yourself if it is 100 percent true, 100 percent of the time. If you shared this thought with 100 strangers, would every single one of them agree? For example, imagine adamantly professing your belief that you're not attractive enough to go on dates—would everyone unanimously agree with your perception of yourself? (Beauty is in the eye of the beholder, remember that one?) Something pretty cool happens when you stop clinging to every belief you have—you recognize that you have a choice to either allow a thought to negatively influence you, or find a more realistic and supportive way of talking to yourself instead.

Here are three tips for evaluating your thoughts:

1. When a thought arises, ask yourself if there is an emotion present. Remember that not only do your emotions influence you, but they can also distort and manipulate your thoughts.

2. Embrace the science. Thoughts are simply electricity in the brain, one neuron firing off after the next, so take this buzzing chatter with a grain of salt. Your thoughts contain information that's worth listening to, but that doesn't mean you have to do what they say.

3. Put some space between the "I" in your thought and you. Instead of saying, "I know I'm going to fail," try saying, "I am having the thought that I'm going to fail." It helps the brain not get caught up in the negativity.

TAKING THOUGHTS LESS SERIOUSLY

When you have a negative thought, grab your journal or phone and write it down. Then, follow it with three ways you can disprove it. Here's an example:

Thonught: *I'm never going to meet someone.*

Couter:

1. *I cannot tell the future; therefore, I cannot prove this is true.*

2. *If I asked my close friends, they would tell me it's still possible.*

3. *Meeting someone is an intersection of many components, not a result of what's happened thus far.*

Further fact-checking:

What story does this thought uphold? (For example, I'm unworthy of love.)

Why am I so quick to agree with this thought? (Maybe because talking shit to myself is my expertise!)

How does believing this thought affect my life? (Keeps me from exploring dating options.)

What would be different if I no longer believed it to be true? (I would exude more self-confidence and possibly attract better humans into my life.)

4. "I can never be in the moment"

You're not alone in that, friend. I still lose myself in anxious thoughts about what I'll wear on trips I haven't even *booked* yet.

For nearly all of us, the present moment is an enigmatic, elusive oasis of the mind. Our mind is wired to wander thanks to a set of brain structures that make up the *default mode network* (Mantini and Vanduffel 2013). We live on an autopilot setting: negatively obsessing about ourselves, remaining stuck in the past, and being anxious about our future. Much of our default mode is steeped in negativity and fear—indeed, our mind's resting state does not feel restful in the least.

We ruminate on what we should have, could have, would have done in the interview for the job we didn't get and beat ourselves up for having procrastinated yet again. When we travel, we mourn having to go home before we even get to our first hotel. Instead of enjoying the movie with our friend, we're in our heads wondering about the "right time" to text a new love interest back. We turn our heads and frantically ask what just happened.

The more our minds wander, the more details of life we miss out on because we aren't paying attention. Negative thoughts are most likely to flood in while we're running on autopilot, which keeps us from being present long enough to practice adaptive, thoughtful self-talk.

MAKING ROOM FOR MINDFULNESS

Distraction, inattention, and getting lost in the past and future all have dire consequences. When we spend much of our lives lost in thought, we're left at the mercy of the content of those thoughts. "*Mindfulness* is the practice of paying attention [to the world] in a particular way: on purpose, in the present moment, and nonjudgmentally" (Kabat-Zinn 2005, 4). To be *mindful of your mind* means to acknowledge what is happening right now by observing your thoughts as they come and go, noticing how they fluctuate based on your emotional state, and noting the valence (pleasant, unpleasant, or neutral). The present moment is where we grow our self-awareness, without which positive change cannot occur.

With dedicated practice, the ability to intentionally bring our attention to the present moment becomes more reflexive and allows us to intentionally direct our mind's eye. We can only address our faulty thinking patterns if we catch ourselves in the act (of talking shit) and do something about it right then and there.

Mindfulness creates a space where we can observe ourselves with clarity and acceptance. As we get to know the familiar cues that prompt maladaptive habits of the mind and are able to respond without judgment, we will develop the ability to free ourselves from the shackles of negativity bias.

Make no mistake, however—intentionally redirecting our awareness over and over again, away from what our brain evolved to focus on, is no easy task. We must keep choosing to engage fully with our environment, instead of wishing we could go back in time or somehow protect ourselves perfectly from the uncertainty of the future.

THE MAGIC OF MINDFULNESS

…allows us to acknowledge the presence of any discomfort or negativity without adding stress by judging our experience. Judging our thoughts, feelings, and behaviors only intensifies stress and negativity.

…helps us accept things as they are without getting caught up in the storyline. Seeing things exactly as they are gives us the freedom to let go of aspects of the story that are no longer serving us.

…improves emotion regulation. We are better able to notice when our thoughts rekindle negative emotions. Slowing down will help us not get carried away by the intensity of a difficult emotional experience.

…encourages self-compassion. When we are mindful of our suffering, we can choose to offer ourselves kindness instead of self-judgment. This profoundly changes the way that we relate to ourselves, and ultimately, the positive effects trickle down to every aspect of our being.

…improves connection in relationships. Our ability to nonjudgmentally observe the way we behave in relationships helps our ego not get in the way when conflict or difficulty comes up. Instead, we more easily self-reflect and improve our communication.

PRACTICING YOUR MAGIC

Here are some ways to bring mindfulness into your life:

- Repeatedly catch your mind any time it wanders. Utilize a practice like deep breathing, a physical activity like stretching, or just naming objects in your environment to bring your mind back to the present moment.

- Consciously take little moments to be away from your electronics. Choose to reconnect with your body by walking or stretching, engage in a more thoughtful activity (for example, knitting, puzzles, watering plants), or pet your sweet animal child.

- Cultivate mindfulness in moments of enjoyment. It is easier to be present when we do something we love or have fun doing because our mind more readily exits autopilot. Next time you're doing a favorite activity, pause to revel in the sensations of pleasure, gratitude, and joy.

- Take moments to acknowledge the person in front of you by really connecting with them. Try actively listening, locking eyes, or noticing something about them in that very moment.

- Meditate! Through consistent meditation, we learn how to observe our inner narrative without judging the content. Soon we realize we have all the power to free ourselves from the shackles of shitty self-talk. I can promise you that five to ten minutes of practice a day will change your relationship to both your outer and inner worlds for the better.

PRO TIP: Mindfulness is most effective if you aim to live more mindfully throughout each day, as opposed to whipping out a practice only when shit goes down. While the idea of meditation overwhelms many, remember that the capacity and ability to engage with the present moment already lie within us. The beauty of mindfulness is it can be practiced at any moment, in any environment, and in any situation.

5. "I just know the worst will happen"

By the time I entered college, I was fluent in worst-case scenario—though regrettably it wasn't a language I could add to my résumé. On the day of orientation, there had been an unusual, dull pain in my sternum all day. By nightfall, the catastrophic thoughts were suddenly accompanied by cold sweats and shallow breathing. I was sure I was having a heart attack. White as a sheet, I walked into the living room and asked my host to call an ambulance. The paramedics clocked my resting heart rate at 190 bpm. It was just a panic attack, they said.

More panic attacks plagued me in months to come, but instead of speaking to myself in self-soothing ways, I only strengthened the habit of scaring myself. My mind regularly filled to the brim with visions of strokes and rare diseases (meningitis was a go-to) any time I felt an unfamiliar twinge in my body, convinced that death was at my door. I didn't know how to cope with the fear in a way that didn't end with hours spent on diagnosing myself online. If a catastrophizing competition had existed, I would have surely podiumed.

Although my story is an example of an extreme version of this thinking trap, zero out of 10 people would not recommend spending any kind of energy robbing yourself of the present by spooking yourself about possible catastrophes in the future.

BECOMING MORE REALISTIC

Those of us who think catastrophically also tend to magnify the severity of our struggles and exaggerate our inability to cope. Phrases like "I won't be able to handle it," "I won't be okay," or "I just know I'll lose it" imply that we are powerless over our future behaviors.

Understanding exactly *why* we have a habit of assuming the worst can help us choose the path of resilience, instead of reinforcing helplessness. For instance, does it give you a sense of control over an uncertain future? Do you believe that if you envision the shittiest outcome, then you can prepare yourself and it won't destroy you if it happens? Are you fearful of being lulled into complacency by believing something good can happen?

Try as we might, we cannot control the future and it would benefit us to stop acting as though we can miraculously hack the space-time continuum by conjuring up potential disasters. It is normal to crave a sense of safety in a world where there is much to be frightened of. However, there are more effective ways to create a sense of peace in the present moment than exhausting ourselves or wasting precious moments of life preparing for something that may or may not come.

Below is a road map detailing how to engage in realistic self-talk that ditches the habit of dreading calamity. When addressing an out-of-control worry, follow these steps in succession or work with one that feels particularly accessible at the time:

1. First, we must fully accept that uncomfortable, unpleasant, and even terrifying things do happen in life whether we like it or not. While it is human to fear the unknown, expecting the worst does not prevent the worst from occurring.

2. Practice catching yourself in a moment of catastrophic thinking. Recognize that even at its scariest, a thought is just a mental event (not a psychic prediction)—and label it *thinking*. Noting thoughts helps our brain not give them so much power.

3. Once labeled, respond to an irrational thought with reassurance instead of more fear. Use a comforting inner voice to say, *Ah yes, there goes my irrational brain yet again. I'm safe right now, there is no need to prepare.*

4. Spend some time writing down every negative outcome to a situation and a corresponding response with a more realistic ending. This will give you alternate responses next time you start thinking the worst will happen.

5. As you write out the more realistic endings, envision successfully coping with and overcoming the worst-case scenario. Humans have time and time again remained resilient in the face of adversity, catastrophe, and significant hardship. You will too.

6. "I'll surely fail, so why bother trying"

Imagine this scenario: you're scrolling through job listings and land on what looks like your dream job. You read over the requirements, and you generally fit the role with a few small exceptions.

That's always when the inner critic butts in—there's no way you'll get the job because you're not the "perfect" candidate. You tell yourself that you're up against people who have more experience than you. You talk a little more shit about how you'd have sucked at the interview anyway, and silently comfort yourself, knowing that by not trying, you won't have to cope with the pain of rejection.

Not trying is one way of assuring certainty in an uncertain world. Fearing potential embarrassment or shame, we predict the worst to avoid trying and possibly confronting these brutal emotions. When our predictions are a reflection of low self-esteem, our self-talk turns critical and demoralizing, paralyzing us.

A pervasive fear of failure permeates every sphere. We don't get a gym membership because we convince ourselves that we won't be able to stick to a routine. We pass on a challenging class despite our interest in it because we believe that we won't be smart enough to succeed. We don't swipe right on someone we think is cute, certain they won't choose us back.

Putting in minimal effort or not trying at all means we don't need to confront that we failed or were rejected because we weren't _____ enough. When I was applying to PhD programs, I knew that I didn't have the years of experience typically required. I avoided proofreading my application essays because some part of me wanted the option to pawn off a rejection onto uninspired writing. For the record, I didn't get accepted into any programs that year and survived to tell the tale.

The fear of failure is part of the human condition, fitting in neatly with our evolutionary drive for survival—for our ancestors, coming back empty-handed after a hunt meant risking starvation. But failing is an inevitable part of being alive, and we'd be foolish to keep trying to avoid it.

When we talk ourselves out of trying at all, we limit our potential. Without taking chances, it is neither possible to build confidence in our abilities nor to learn how to recover from life's pitfalls. It takes a lot of courage to let go of predicting shitty outcomes and to stop magnifying what failure will feel like. Being courageous doesn't mean fear evaporates—we just need to wholeheartedly know that we can endure that pit-in-the-stomach, heat-in-our-face, burning-behind-our-eyes sensation that arises when we inevitably face our shortcomings.

TRANSFORMING YOUR
RELATIONSHIP TO FAILURE

Redefine failure to change your perspective and make it less scary as a possibility. "Failure" is a loaded word, but it doesn't have to be. A baby learning to walk wobbles and falls many times before they take their full first steps. Scientists have many failed experiments before something works. Choose to see failure as a learning experience every time.

Trust that you can handle an undesirable outcome. Low self-worth or self-esteem can convince us that we can't take another blow. However, we're working hard on that, aren't we? Your body and mind are highly capable of tolerating levels of discomfort. Failure won't kill you, nor does it have to tank your self-image.

Choose not to define your identity by your failures no matter how many times they happen, just as you would not define anyone else based on theirs. Think of someone you respect who has objectively failed at something and consider how you feel toward them. Do you judge their lack of success, or do you admire their willingness to try?

Remember: We did not learn to fear failure in a vacuum—the expectations of others play a subconscious role in our self-consciousness. Luckily, most people are too busy worrying about themselves to care whether you succeed or not. You're your own harshest critic. When people in your life judge your hit-or-miss rate, perhaps it's time to reevaluate their influence on your life.

PRO TIP: Teach yourself to think *So what?* any time you visualize defeat. The more casually we think about the outcome, the easier we will convince ourselves that it truly doesn't matter what happens.

7. "Reality blows"

Yes, it does, and you are not alone in thinking that, dear friend. Reality can be a bitch sometimes and we'll do just about anything to avoid it.

Contrary to the way this word is often used, *acceptance* does not mean giving in, giving up, or settling. Acceptance is the act of acknowledging or noticing reality in the present moment, without judging it or trying to change it in any way, even in our minds. It doesn't mean we have to like or love things as they are.

However, this is exactly where the difficulty arises—we insist on a reality that's pleasant and without discomfort. We *want* to like or love it so that we can exist in peace, instead of in dissonance or aversion. Suffering arises when we want reality to be anything other than what it is.

A very simple example is when we get frustrated because the train has not arrived yet. Are you one of the folks who leans over the edge of the platform to see if you can see the headlights coming? Perhaps I've seen you; I like to stand where I can observe the restlessness of the underground, all while I practice leaning into what is true: the train has not yet arrived, no matter how much I may need or want it to.

Struggling to accept reality is a more covert form of unhelpful self-talk; it does not necessarily take the shape of unkind words. Dwelling on how much we dislike how things are in the present moment keeps us stuck in the past or an alternate, uncontrollable vision of our present. The more emotional valence something has, the more difficult it tends to be to accept as our current truth.

For example, when we experience loss of any kind—friendship, breakup, death, or time—acceptance can seem impossible, offensive if even suggested. Our mind stays stuck attempting to stave off the pain of having to exist in a new reality. For as long as we wish for things we cannot change to be different, we will experience some form of suffering—whether it comes in the shape of denial, distraction, longing, or agony.

RADICAL ACCEPTANCE OF REALITY

When we *radically* accept something difficult in our life, we stop resisting our present reality with our whole mind, body, and heart (Brach 2004). I like to imagine that radical acceptance feels like floating in the Dead Sea; it is the moment we let the tension in our body go and allow the salt to cradle us at the surface. There is nothing that we need to do; only be.

How humans tend to react to distress:

1. We try to change the circumstances.

2. We try to change our behavior to cope with the circumstances.

3. We continue to feel miserable or poorly.

4. We accept the circumstances.

Reminders for Radical Acceptance:

1. Reality is what it is and we cannot change it, no matter how unpleasant or difficult.

2. There are causes and reasons for the reality that we're experiencing or living through.

3. Although the experience of pain is inescapable, we can prevent or lessen the experience of suffering.

PRACTICING ACCEPTANCE

Write down an event that happened in your life that has caused you stress or pain. Explore why it is difficult for you to accept. Ask yourself if you can go back in time and change your response. (Hint: you don't have access to a time machine.)

Write out your acceptance statement(s). For example: *I accept that the friendship is over*. Practice saying the acceptance statement out loud with a firm and confident tone and write the statement down so you can use it as a reminder at any point. Repeat often.

While practicing, take deep breaths (in through the nose, out through the mouth) while you consciously relax muscle groups throughout your body. A calmer body is a less resistant body; a less resistant body is a less resistant mind.

PRO TIP: If at any time you find yourself thinking, *But I don't accept it*, answer the following questions: What are the bare, hard facts of what happened? Leave perceptions, opinions, and judgments out of it, and ask, Did it happen in my reality? Say "yes" neutrally, not begrudgingly. If I hear tone, I ask my client to try again. Finally end by saying, "Yes, it is part of my reality." Ta-da!

8. "Separating from my thoughts and emotions feels impossible"

Thoughts and emotions can be overwhelming and ruthlessly convincing. However, our struggle lies not in their content or potency, but rather in our maladaptive reaction to our experience of them. Instead of treating them simply as information, we tend to *over-identify* with our thinking and feeling which only amplifies a negative state of mind or mood. This means that we get caught up in the meaning of thoughts and the intensity of emotions to an excessive degree instead of viewing these inner experiences with an objective lens. In those moments, we become fused with what we're thinking or feeling, making it difficult to have the perspective necessary for making wise and rational decisions. Additionally, over-identification makes things feel permanent, even though they're entirely transient.

As humans, our sense of self is a crucial part of our experience; therefore, it is often a struggle to separate ourselves from self-proclaimed (and assigned) identities and roles we inhabit. Elements of our personality, career path, or behavior, for example, become the entirety of who we are instead of just a piece of a complex puzzle.

If we struggle with anxiety, we might call ourselves an "anxious person" instead of thinking of ourselves as someone who *gets* anxious. If we are bullied for our appearance or weight, we may grow up struggling to define ourselves in any other way. If someone tells us that they don't love us back, then we believe we're "unlovable" because we've taken on someone else's opinion of ourselves, and more self-defeating chatter quickly follows suit.

Talking to ourselves this way is harmful for a few reasons: it can further solidify an already faulty core belief (I've been broken up with three times. There must be something wrong with me); it can take away our power through labeling (I don't just *think* I'm inadequate. I *am* inadequate); and it signals to our brain that change will not be possible because it's who we *are* (I've always reacted like this—it's just how I am).

Much of my Russian family thought I was "too much"—too outspoken, too emotional, too sensitive; they let me know it, too. I became self-conscious of my expressiveness, and hangouts with friends were riddled with relentless worry that I had been too loud or talked too much.

I *did* have a lot to say, and I *was* quite passionately loud at times, but I couldn't let go of the fear that my friends secretly found me intolerable. I started quieting myself so as to not expose who I convinced myself I was: an obnoxious, overly effusive, overwhelming human. What started as a criticism given by those uncomfortable with my vulnerability (of course I didn't know that then) became a set of fear-driven thoughts that I adopted as my identity.

DEVELOPING MINDFUL AWARENESS

When we have overidentified with a thought or belief, we need mindful awareness to interrupt the overidentification process. Mindfulness practice requires nonjudgment and a balanced approach to negative experiences, both internal and external. When we are mindful, we neither ignore nor exaggerate our thoughts or emotions. Remember that despite the intensity a feeling can create in our body, and despite how easily a moment of shitty self-image takes over, these are passing, impermanent states. They are *not* representative of our entire being.

Our minds in default mode can be drama queens. For example, if you find out a colleague has been talking behind your back, your reflex may be to feel overcome with a difficult emotion like embarrassment or anger. In seconds, you're in a spiral over whether what you said to them during a work meeting was taken the wrong way. Instead, make it your goal not to give meaning or power to their perception of you. Instead of personalizing their shit-talking, you can instead choose to simply be aware of the person's behavior without getting too upset or allowing it to infiltrate your sense of self.

Our self-talk will transform once we recognize that we take ourselves (thoughts, feelings, sensations) too seriously. But it's not enough to understand the concept, we must embody the philosophy by reminding ourselves that a negative inner dialogue and difficult emotions can be questioned, ignored, reframed, observed, or accepted, which are all often better options than fusing to them. It is powerful to know that like the weather, we cannot control the phenomena that the mind produces: sometimes it rains, sometimes it snows, and sometimes the sun shines. It just *is*. (Kindly suspend existential panic about climate change.)

PRO TIP: *Drop the "I."* Try talking to yourself in third person by saying, "You are having the thought that you are unlikeable." Your brain is more objective in this state, giving you the space not to become your thoughts or emotions.

GAINING PERSPECTIVE

Grab a piece of paper and separate it into three sections: *Situation*, *Overidentification*, and *Eagle Eye*. (An eagle flies high up in the sky and gets a zoomed-out picture of the earth below. Use this as a way to help your brain create more space and objectivity. Any other bird will work, too.)

Now, practice recognizing your own experience of overidentification. Think of a recent situation that caused you distress. In the first section, describe the situation in detail. In the second section, describe aspects of the situation you have overidentified with (such as a triggered core belief or fear) and how you speak to yourself about it. In the last section, zoom out to describe the situation from an objective view.

Here is an example:

Situation: *My friend didn't text me back when I asked them to hang out, which isn't typical of them. Lately, they've been spending a lot of time with a work friend I've only met briefly a couple of times. My fear of not being good enough flares up and I wonder if maybe my friend doesn't want to be pals anymore since they have someone new.*

Overidentified self-talk: *They have been my best friend since high school. We used to do everything together and now they met this person at their job, and suddenly they haven't been spending nearly as* much time with me. Their coworker is probably way more fun to be around than me since I often am struggling with anxiety. They still haven't responded to my text this morning and I feel like they probably are realizing they don't really want to be friends with me anymore.

Objective view: This is my best friend and they have been for almost ten years. We went to college together and they've always been there for me. We just hung out a couple of nights ago and it was awesome. Even though we're both busy with work, we've been able to see a good amount of each other. If they didn't text back, they probably have a normal reason for it as I don't have any evidence that they would just abandon me. I can also be happy that they are getting along with someone at their job, where I know they felt a bit isolated until now.

In this example, the person is taking innocent pieces of their experience (their best friend has a new friend and they're late to text) and extrapolating information such that now they have a narrative about being less valued in their friendship. Instead, they would benefit from stepping back and realizing that it's normal for people to make new friends and how one missing text doesn't need to impact their self-esteem this much.

9. "I can't stop thinking about this"

I still get seriously peeved when I remember that the brain's best shot at solving the unsolvable is ruminating on the same shit over and over again.

One of the functions of our thought loops is that they give us an illusory sense of control over a situation that otherwise feels upsetting, unfinished, or uncertain. Our brain can tirelessly play out past scenarios and future worries, to try to protect us from the intolerable discomfort of not knowing.

Thinking loops often prevent us from accepting the reality of something that perhaps we don't feel ready or willing to accept yet. It can feel good to indulge in the repetitive thoughts because it makes us feel that we can somehow solve, correct, go back in time, reaffirm, or reassure ourselves. But it's ineffective and exhausting.

Let's just imagine how much time we could get back if we didn't endlessly replay conversations in our mind or if we allowed a situation to unfold without dreading an outcome for days—I think I'd get back at least three years.

UNSTICK YOURSELF

Remember that when it comes to changing your mental habits, it isn't enough to *understand* that your thoughts aren't always true nor helpful information. The challenge is in *changing the habit* of saying things to yourself—learning how to regularly catch yourself in the act of thinking loops and shifting gears.

When you notice yourself stuck in a thought loop, it can be helpful to ask what the function of the rumination is in that given moment. Humans typically ruminate on:

- A problem that can't necessarily be solved

- A past experience or behavior that feels unresolved, uncomfortable, or one that we wish we could re-experience to double-check what we did or said

- Thoughts that involve planning or thinking ahead about things—details we're worried we will somehow lose or forget if we don't think them over and over again

- Worrying about a future event that we're fearful of or nervous about

However, you've caught on by now that getting stuck in thinking loops doesn't actually serve any of those functions. Quite the opposite, it tires us and makes us spend precious energy suffering instead of practicing acceptance and moving about our day with less anxiety.

UNSTICKING YOURSELF, STEP-BY-STEP

When you notice yourself thinking the same thing over and over, try following these steps:

1. Label what is happening a "thinking loop" or "rumination."

2. Write down as many of the thoughts as you can. Keep the list so that if this particular thought loop returns, you can choose to read it instead of repeating it in your head. Think of it as a log of thoughts you don't want to lose.

3. Reflect on the function of the loop you're in. Are you trying to protect yourself from uncertainty or something potentially painful? Are you fulfilling a need with your thoughts? Like the need to feel heard or validated for something that happened in the past? Is there a problem you're trying to solve?

4. Practice accepting reality as it is. If you're struggling to let go of something in the past, say to yourself *I accept that this happened* with an energy of understanding that you cannot change it. If there's uncertainty that you're having difficulty sitting with, say to yourself *I accept that most of life is uncertain.*

5. Finally, get busy doing something else that's purposeful or enjoyable. Engaging your mind with something in the present that fulfills you will help you exit the loop.

6. Each time you notice the thinking return, give yourself a gentle reminder: *I've thought through this already. No more thinking about it is going to change anything.*

10. "I can't..."

Dear reader, stay vigilant. There's a word we use without restriction that slips into conversation with the stealth of a cat jumping onto your bed to sleep at your feet without even waking you up. Here are a handful of examples we casually throw around:

- I can't do…

- I can't understand why…

- I can't stop thinking about…

- I can't be…

- I can't get myself to…

- I can't imagine…

- I can't let go of…

- I can't figure out how to…

- I can't stop feeling guilty for…

Can't. Our nearly unconscious use of this word doesn't escape our clever brain. Once it registers your words, the brain structure responsible for meaning does a Google search for the definition of *can't* and swiftly obeys your command.

Sometimes, we are genuinely convinced that we can't do something. Two common phrases I hear are, "I've tried to stop thinking about it, but I just can't," or "I can't ever get over this." Notice how with just one word, we strip ourselves of the accountability to put in the effort it will take to make our lives a little easier and our minds a little quieter.

In sessions, I don't miss an opportunity to jump in and say, "You *can* do it. You have the capacity to," first emphasizing the objective meaning of the word, and then asking my client what it is they're really trying to say.

TELL YOURSELF YOU CAN

Once you're easily catching yourself using "can't" in your self-talk, become curious about when you tend to use this word. Is it when you're thinking about the future or the past? Is it connected to when your self-esteem or mood is low? How often have you limited your experiences or growth by saying "can't" when you're more than capable?

Don't forget to assert what you *can* do in the situation. Sometimes things genuinely are out of your control—you've learned by now that this is not the case when it comes to mental habits. Consistent practice of more adaptive, positive language eventually shapes new neural pathways, the way heavy rains will run over bedrock, eventually creating grooves for a river to run through.

SAYING WHAT YOU MEAN

Remember that "I can't" is usually a code for "I don't want to," "I've tried and failed to," "I'm not ready to," "It feels too hard to," or "I'm too scared to."

Let's jump into some examples. The letter *a* represents our can't statement; *b* will be one of many ways we can say what we really mean.

> **a.** I can't get over her/him/them.
>
> **b.** I haven't yet properly processed the pain from that experience, so it's difficult to imagine moving forward.
>
> **a.** I can't be around my parents.
>
> **b.** I want to protect my emotional boundaries by choosing not to spend time with them.
>
> **a.** I can't stop feeling guilty.
>
> **b.** I struggle being self-compassionate toward my mistakes.

Your turn! Follow the format above for five of your own typical *can't* statements. Remember that this sneaky self-talk disempowers, no matter how inconsequential it seems. When in doubt, simply replace "I can't..." with "It's really hard to..."

11. "I should..."

I'm a stickler for language in therapy sessions. I don't waste much time before asking them to drop the sneaky "should" like a hot potato. Sooner or later, most start correcting themselves before I beat them to the punch—they don't want to hear "the speech" again. I throw them a knowing look and a thumbs-up. Everybody wins.

Should is a self-talk series regular; the unexpected villain masquerading as a reminder for us to do or be something:

- I should be healthier/go to the gym/eat better

- I should be more productive/stop procrastinating

- I should be able to get through/do this on my own

- I should get over it

- I should be past this by now

- I should do more/less of (insert desired/undesired habit)

- I should be more original/creative/(insert desired adjective here)

Should implies that there is a better way to be than how you are—and judgment is deserved for not having moved toward change. Often, "should statements" are idealistic and unattainable, therefore making us feel more anxious, inferior, and guilty.

Try not to overthink it, of course—sometimes the S word is just the simplest way to get your point across. However, it doesn't hurt to become more mindful of the instances when you're using it to beat yourself up or ruminate on something you didn't do. Seriously…you shouldn't do that.

SAYING GOODBYE TO SHOULDS

Examine the evidence for and against your "should statement." This is an opportunity for you to explore the truthfulness of your thought. Here's an example: *I should be better at this by now.* What is the evidence indicating that you need to be further ahead? According to whom? What has kept you from being better? Is there a way to get yourself there without putting yourself down?

Accept your shortcomings and embrace your humanness. Of course, there are plenty of moments in our life when doing something differently would have resulted in positive self-growth. However, we would be wise to remember that we are not perfect beings, which means we won't always act in our own best interest—and that's all part of the human condition.

Put down the measuring stick you're using. Often, "should" comes from a place of comparison, and that's not to say that there isn't pressure—social, familial or otherwise—but ultimately, it is *your* choice whether you allow others' experiences, qualities, and flaws to be your measuring guide as to how *you* should be.

Take away the guilt and take accountability. "Should" implies we've done something bad or wrong or haven't done/aren't enough of something. Even if that were the case, what would need to happen to move forward in a better way? If there is something we genuinely want or need to change, guilt can disempower us. Instead, use more motivating language—like "want" or "will"—and notice the impact of dropping the judgment.

Replace "should" with more productive, realistic self-talk. What are you really trying to say? For example, you might think: *I should get over my fear already.* Instead, try saying: *It's pretty normal to be afraid—I'm taking steps to become more courageous. It takes time to change.* A more understanding approach works wonders.

12. "Trying again is too overwhelming after failing"

Sometimes I hold my breath when a patient, still unsure of how to fail without feeling like shit about themselves, tells me the story of a risk they took only to come up short. For many of us, these stories become hard evidence against future attempts, even when we're reminded of the courage it took to be vulnerable without a guaranteed positive outcome. But remember, our inner critic did not learn to thrive in a vacuum—we are conditioned to fear judgment and avoid it when we can.

Let's talk about the stuff of reality TV—romantic failure. It's common knowledge that the dating world (in NYC, at least) can be a demoralizing shitshow for everyone involved, and yet, it's very hard after a certain number of attempts to not start reading into dating flops as personal failures. Defeated, patients and friends alike say, "Whether I keep choosing the wrong people or good ones aren't choosing me, I've clearly got to stop trying." We all flip through the mental Rolodex of evidence: crap dates, plenty of ghosts, and handfuls of rejections. I have five years of online dating fails to look back upon, but I'll save those for a memoir.

Each of us has particular areas in which the stakes are high, our self-image is on the line, and the margin of error between success and failure is razor thin. If our self-esteem is closely linked to outcome, our ability to tolerate the experience of failure is likely very low. Like a mudslide after torrential rain, negative thoughts flood our minds and painful emotions like disappointment, embarrassment, fear, and shame take over. Instead of comforting ourselves, we focus on how much we sucked, who saw us suck, who will find out we suck, and how we will never make the mistake to try again. Thanks to human egocentrism, we believe that others give much more of a shit about our shortcomings than they actually do. Remember that although the fear of failing again can be daunting, it is not worth sacrificing the self-growth that happens only while doing the things that scare us. We're better off following the wisdom of Mr. Beckett:

Try again. Fail again. Fail better.
—Samuel Beckett

HOW TO FAIL BETTER

Try these ways to circumvent fear and change your relationship to failure:

Build awareness. How are you defining failure? Why are you fearful of failing again? Where have you experienced success, however small? Are your goalposts for success reasonable, and realistic? Is there any comparison or perfectionism at play?

Zoom out. Will your failure matter when you're ninety and your dentures fall out as you bend over to water your hydrangeas? Will it even matter in a year? Will those who love you hold it against you?

Normalize failure. Seriously, everybody's doing it. Failing can feel isolating, but it doesn't have to be. Visualize the eight billion people all over the planet all failing at different things at once.

Practice self-compassion. Validate your struggle and offer yourself more of what you need in the given moment to self-soothe. Failing can hurt, and the experience of pain, when met with a compassionate response, will make it more likely that you won't give up on something that's important to you.

Use the moment as your teacher. What did you learn from your failure? Ask yourself every single time something doesn't go your way. What can I take away from this?

Use the flowchart on the next page to help you navigate the experience of failure:

failure flowchart

did you fail at something?

nope! → yeah...

nope! branch:
just a matter of time

yeah... branch:
how do you feel?

like a failure → it's not your entire identity

chillin' hard

that's so true! there are many other facets of me

failing

but i've failed a lot

welcome to the club

you're so right!

it feels like i'll never succeed → you have a crystal ball?

yes → cool! can i borrow it?

well, no...

failing is human! you can simply stop trying, or you can learn from each experience. seeing yourself as a failure only paralyzes you from trying again to "protect" you from the shame of failure — but failing isn't some fundamental flaw.

learn to change your perspective on what it means to fail. some shit doesn't work out. sometimes we're not meant for something. sometimes it takes a bunch of tries. maybe it's not failure, maybe it's just living your life.

got fail?

13. "I guilt myself often"

We're human—sometimes, we fuck up.

More often, we *think* we've fucked up. Nearly always, our mind *magnifies* the fuckup.

Guilt can show up as early as three years of age, during a developmental stage when we start to become conscious of the self (Luby et al. 2009). Guilt is an emotion we feel when we believe or recognize that we did something wrong or harmful. The dissonance we feel is meant to push us to make repairs by apologizing or changing our behavior to demonstrate our understanding of what we did. So, if you do feel guilty now and again, it's probably safe to rule out psychopathy.

One of my darling clients, a sufferer of chronic guilt, always jokes that her mom tells her that she came out of the womb apologizing. A chronic guilt-tripper erroneously suffers under the belief or fear that their behavior hurt another person, or they overestimate how much responsibility they bear for the perceived wrongdoing. Regardless of whether there is a valid reason for feeling guilty, behavior can range from overapologizing to avoidance, in large part stemming from fear of not being perceived as good. When our self-talk encourages us to *know* we are good enough, we won't feel the same overwhelming need to prove our goodness by groveling or punishing ourselves indefinitely.

LET IT GO

The song from *Frozen* has possibly ruined this phrase for many of us, but it's a tried-and-true mantra within our new philosophy when it comes to dealing with guilt. When you do something wrong, allow guilt to be just the temporary emotion needed to take accountability. Stay guilty for too long, and guilt prevents us from engaging in restorative action—we spend more time blaming ourselves than doing something about it.

In case you *didn't* do anything wrong, and you still feel guilt, here's a flowchart for you to follow:

14. "Being kind to myself isn't an option"

I often wonder, when did self-kindness go out of style? Was it ever *in*? We flog ourselves with critical, unforgiving words any time we think we suck. If we didn't go to the gym just like we said we would, we're lazy and unable to commit. If we let our partner down and they express their disappointment, we question whether we deserve them. If we make a mistake at work, we're stupid and unskilled. If we take a while to recover from heartbreak, we're pathetic for still caring. To ensure we feel like shit, all we need to do is to keep talking shit.

Whether you've always known how much you judge yourself or you're just realizing it now, lack of kindness toward yourself has plenty of potential origins.

- We believe self-kindness won't be as motivating as self-judgment.

- We believe we'll never learn from our mistakes if we don't criticize ourselves.

- We are conditioned to believe that we do not deserve kindness.

- We think that if we say something mean to ourselves first, no one else can tell us something that we don't already know.

- We find comfort in the familiarity of self-punishing language.

- We're afraid to be vulnerable by acknowledging ourselves with kindness.

Whatever your reason is for leaving self-kindness out of your self-talk repertoire, you can't expect your mind to help you build healthy habits or self-esteem if you're busy battering yourself each chance you get. You have a choice of self-talk: one option brings you closer to your best self; the other keeps you down in the mud under a boot. Yes, it's one of the hardest habits of the mind to break—but it will be fucking worth it.

READING SUGGESTION:

Pick up a copy of Christopher Germer and Kristin Neff's *Mindful Self-Compassion Workbook*; Germer and Neff are pioneers in self-kindness practice, and much of my learning, and the foundation of these exercises, is credited to their having paved the way.

RESPONDING WITH SELF-KINDNESS

Lack of forgiveness causes almost all of our self-sabotaging behavior.
—Mark Victor Hansen

For years, destructive thoughts about my body relentlessly hounded me. My best friend knew my struggle intimately, and often tried to help turn the volume down on my inner critic by showing me—and my body—unconditional kindness.

The greatest gift she'd given me was her response one day when I had said something overtly mean about my thighs. With the expert, playful reprimand of a lovable elementary schoolteacher, she said "Hey, don't you dare say that about my best friend!" I was disarmed, my brain taking a few moments to work out the profoundness of what she'd said.

The shit we say to ourselves when we're struggling or unhappy or we fuck up is not what we would say to our loved ones, or even to a new crush we met online. Instead, we are supportive and understanding, offering reassuring reasons why they're wrong to beat themselves up. To practice self-kindness, use the following exercise as a template for your own personal examples:

PRACTICING SELF-KINDNESS

Consider a recent time you've been particularly hard on yourself. Get out your journal and write out the situation. Then write out what your critical inner voice is telling you about the situation. Finally, write out what it would look like to reframe the situation with self-kindness.

Here is an example:

Situation: *I'm in a relationship and my partner is following their purpose and in a career path they're really happy with. Meanwhile, I don't like my job and haven't found what area makes me happy.*

Critical voice: *I should have figured out what I want to do by now, but the major that I chose in college was useless. I'm not an equal and I can barely contribute to this relationship. I'm sure my partner thinks that I'm lazy and pathetic. I hate my job, but I don't have any skills to do anything else.*

Self-kindness reframe: *I'm surrounded by people who struggle to figure out what they want to do. There is objectively no timeline to follow in life. I'm grateful that I'm with someone who is doing something they love, and it's something I can look up to instead of beating myself up about.*

Self-kindness on-the-go tip: *Whether you're angry, stressed, guilty, depressed, or overwhelmed, ask yourself, What would I say to my best friend (or favorite pet or family member) if this was them?*

15. "This is just who/how I am"

Arguably, the biggest challenge as a therapist is to support a person in successfully changing their *core belief*—a deep-seated, strongly held perception of the self. It can be maddening to have a standoff with someone's core belief because it typically has had years of conditioning—whereas I just met it (an unfair matchup, if you ask me). I have some clients who are Olympic level at poking holes in any of my attempts to disprove their subjective truth. This is because self-views are maintained by our tendency to get stuck on evidence that confirms the belief and to ignore any evidence that contradicts it.

Core beliefs can negatively influence the way we interpret life experiences and what people say to us. They become harmful when we *accept* them as fact, whether or not they are true. If we take the time to explore one belief we have about ourselves (for example, "I am flawed"), we can also begin to see what areas of our life this has negatively affected (maybe you strive for unattainable perfection and give up if you don't think you can achieve it).

Here are some of the most common core beliefs. If any resonate, I want you to hear this loud and clear: they are only true because you continue *choosing* to believe them.

I am a failure.	I can't do it.	I am incompetent.
I am a loser.	I am insignificant.	I will fail.
I am flawed.	I am broken.	I am weak.
I can't succeed.	I am ugly.	I am not good enough.
I am nothing.	I can't change.	I am a bad person.
I am invisible.	I am inferior.	I am not lovable.
I am powerless.	I am unlikeable.	I am not enough.
I am stupid.	I am unattractive.	I am not safe.
I am all alone.	I am needy.	I am not special.
I am unimportant.	I don't deserve success.	I'm a failure.
I am a burden.	I am crazy.	I am worthless.
I don't matter.	I'm uninteresting.	I am useless.
I am a mistake.	I am unfixable.	I don't measure up.
I don't deserve to be happy.	I am guilty.	I am unsuccessful.
		I don't belong.

These are all total bullshit, just FYI.

BELIEVING SOMETHING ELSE

Even if beliefs *feel* very true to us, we are allowed to change them any time we want because they are ultimately mind-made perceptions. Since we aren't taught to question their logic nor to explore other possibilities of what might be true, beliefs take root and become harder to dig up the longer we cling to and live by them. It can take a construction-grade excavator to pull them out.

At any point, we are capable of believing something else, especially when our belief harms and limits us. We may initially feel as though we're lying to ourselves as we work on adopting a more adaptive mindset. That's totally normal when you're in the midst of changing a habit, so keep practicing; in time, your new truth will start to bloom.

CHANGING YOUR BELIEFS

In this exercise, choose one of your limiting core beliefs. Then create your own new core belief that is both self-accepting and true (aka not based entirely on biased self-perceptions). Grab your journal and use the following example to guide you.

Experience: *I go to therapy and I'm on medication for my depression, but nothiit's not everything about me; someone who liked me wouldn't judge mng has changed in my dating life. I can't seem to get past a few dates because I don't think anyone wants to be with someone who has this much baggage. I just can't imagine meeting anyone who would actually want to be with someone this fucked-up.*

Limiting core belief: *There is something fundamentally wrong with me. I'm meant to be alone.*

New balanced core belief: *I am imperfect, like all humans. I have depression, but e for it. It is difficult to feel rejected, but it's likely that I just haven't met the right person. No one deserves to be alone—it takes time and luck to meet your person.*

Remember that our core beliefs are too simplified to be entirely backed up by objective evidence; practicing this exercise will remind you that we are complex creatures who can't logically be defined by a shitty adjective or two. This means that when it no longer serves us, we can use a more flexible approach to view our ever-evolving sense of self.

16. "If only I could change the past"

Like a coach playing back a tape to analyze what happened in a losing game, we push the rewind button over and over again. At some point, there is no new information we can gather by reliving what has happened, and yet we feel an impulse to play through a situation one more time.

We replay conversations, trying to make sure we didn't say something foolish or annoying. We replay fights, imagining the different ways we should have phrased our angry words. We press rewind on moments in a recently ended relationship, as though we think we'll catch the very moment that caused its demise.

Unfortunately, we must face the fact that we cannot go back in time, no matter how much our brain tries. On top of the exhaustion of rumination marathons, our memories become a source of blame and regret. *They broke up with me because I asked too much of them—I knew I was too clingy. I sounded so awkward when I introduced myself—they probably thought I was weird.*

Sometimes, we scavenge the past to search for clues that will not solve any mystery. Other times, we're fearful of letting go, and believe that moving forward would mean never finding the closure we seek. From an evolutionary perspective, it makes a lot of sense that we relentlessly rack our brains to search for any errors in judgment that could compromise our survival.

Lucky for us, we don't have to find more clever ways to forage for berries without disturbing dangerous wildlife. The worst thing that can happen if we choose the present is that we'll have to confront things as they are, which is never as treacherous as it feels, even if it isn't always pleasant.

SOAKING UP THE PRESENT

The present is where contentment and joy live because we can only fully experience these emotions when we are paying attention to them. No amount of time travel—especially when we're emotionally charged up—will offer us the answers, the safety, nor the control we are often desperate for.

The following practice will strengthen your mindfulness skills, which will eventually help you form the habit of more regularly catching yourself reliving the past.

RETURNING TO THE PRESENT

Step 1: Find a comfortable seat. You're welcome to lie down, but know that it can sometimes turn into naptime. Set a timer for five to ten minutes.

Step 2: *Close your eyes and take a few slow, deep breaths, filling up your belly and lungs. Bring to mind something that happened in the past that still bothers you or is keeping you stuck. Think about it in detail.*

Step 3: *After you've thoroughly played through the scenario, return to paying attention to your breath, focusing on the sensation of air entering your nose. When you catch your mind wandering, bring the awareness back to the base of your nostrils.*

Step 4: *Every so often, notice any thoughts about the situation from the past. Notice any new body sensations or emotions that arise.*

Step 5: Continue to practice shifting awareness, oscillating between your breath and your thoughts of the past.

Practice will slowly rewire the habit of getting stuck talking to yourself about events in the past. Remember that you can always rely on curiosity, acceptance, and self-compassion to aid you in the process of coming back to the now.

let go of all attempts
to hold on to the past,
and all desires to
look into the future;
it is only in the
present where peace
truly exists

17. "I hate the uncertainty"

I've always had a plan for my life. By thirteen, having let go of my dreams of being a professional clown or actress, I became certain that I wanted to be a psychologist. My next fifteen years were planned out: APs, BS, MA, and PhD in clinical psychology, licensed with a specialty in adolescent eating disorder treatment, married by twenty-five to my college sweetheart, a cool mom by twenty-six, and a private practice by thirty.

It turned out that my perfectionistic approach to my future was laughable, as life has a knack for mixing things up whether you like it or not. In response, I developed a habit of obsessing over the minutiae of the future to offset my discomfort of life's unpredictability.

Looking back, it comes as no surprise that it wasn't the years-long anxiety about the unknown nor the many mental trips to the future that were the saving grace of my life's path. Instead, it was a combination of motivation, effort, timing, and luck that influenced my life's unfolding.

That said, at the very least, my experiences made me a relatable figure in my therapeutic interactions with today's twenty-somethings, who live in a near-constant state of anxiety about various issues that range from achieving financial independence to finding their purpose with a college degree they deem irrelevant. These days, much of my efforts involve teaching skills aimed at letting go of their desperate attempts to control the uncontrollable.

RETURNING TO THE NOW

When I teach mindfulness, most everyone questions how they could possibly be present in a world ruled by deadlines, precious, limited vacation days, and retirement planning. Students have a "gotcha!" air about them, as though they have caught me in an elaborate lie. I explain that planning, anticipating, or preparing isn't inherently *bad*. It is that alongside our largely futile attempts to tolerate and control life's uncertainty by way of anxious, future-oriented self-talk, we must continuously return to the present to *enjoy* the life we worry about so much.

So, the next time you're getting too caught up in self-talk drenched in apprehension, anticipation, dread, or plain ol' worry, try a little ask-and-answer sesh using the following example:

Q: How am I living in the future?

A: I'm worried about my upcoming beach vacation getting rained out, so I keep thinking of how much it will suck.

• • •

Q: What *purpose* does this state of mind serve?

A: By continuously checking the weather forecast, it feels like I can keep my anxiety somewhat at bay. It says it's going to rain for part of my trip and I'm hoping it will change every time I look at it.

• • •

Q: What am I missing as a result of living in the future?

A: I haven't been able to feel excited for my first vacation in a year because I'm dreading potentially bad weather ruining it altogether.

Q: What do I fear will happen if I were to let it go for some time?

A: It feels as if the more I look at it, the more likely it will be that the weather will change. If I stop checking, I'll just keep worrying that the weather will suck. At least by checking, I have *some* information.

• • •

Q: How can I connect with what is happening *right now*?

A: I can recognize that no amount of staring at a weather app will give me control over whether it ends up raining. I will have to accept it if it does because I'm not canceling this trip. Every time I get the impulse to check the weather, I can instead engage in a tactile exercise with an object within my reach. I'll use it as an opportunity to become mindful of where I am at this moment, not where I will be a week from now.

18. "I'm a shitty person"

Whether we name-call ourselves using explicit or nonexplicit language ("piece of shit" or "idiot," for example), these attempts at character assassination are about as wretched as self-talk gets. This is because beliefs that we are "bad" enter into the territory of arguably the most insidious emotion of all: shame.

Shame is defined by shame researcher and storyteller Brené Brown as the "intensely painful feeling or experience of believing that we are flawed and therefore unworthy of acceptance and belonging" (Brown 2007, 5). Shame can underlie core beliefs; conversely, it can also become a consequence of having a habit of unchecked self-blame and self-criticism. Shame's wrath convinces us that we are fundamentally unworthy, unlovable, or unacceptable the way we are; it makes us fear that the things we've done or failed to do will disconnect us from others or make us undeserving of connection in the first place.

Chronic or intense guilt sometimes masks the more treacherous emotion of shame. Shame creeps up when you point the guilt at yourself and allow it to become part of who you *are*.

Brené Brown, Christopher Germer, and Kristen Neff, all experts in the ruthless emotion, describe in their work some well-researched and helpful truths about shame. First, shame itself is not a "bad" emotion but rather one that comes out of our deep-seated (and very human!) desire to be accepted. Second, if we experience shame, we are not alone. Shame is experienced by almost everyone at some point. But in the end, it is simply an emotion, and all emotions are temporary (Germer 2009; Neff and Germer 2018.)

Shame is so potent because it strongly activates our nervous system and begs for any action that will alleviate how isolating it feels. Unfortunately, many of those actions take the form of self-punishment, self-judgment, avoidance, and even self-harm. The more shame we feel, the more we want to hide (or sometimes, lash out), which only magnifies the pain of loneliness created by our perceived "unworthiness" and "nonbelonging." I won't underplay the immense challenge of changing our relationship to shame, but as we learn how to become more resilient to it, we will experience the most authentic connection to ourselves and others.

PRACTICING SELF-COMPASSION

To have compassion for someone, we must see they are suffering, express our understanding of the pain, and feel moved to alleviate it (even if we can't). It also means accepting suffering as a part of the human condition. *Self-compassion* is the act of turning that loving energy toward ourselves when we are struggling, noticing something we dislike about ourselves, feeling difficult emotions, or are in any state of distress or discomfort (Germer 2009).

To practice self-compassion, we must pause to validate our pain and ask how we can comfort and take care of ourselves in that moment. With a more balanced and kinder approach, our mind feels safer to adopt more realistic beliefs about who we are.

Let's dispel a common myth here: self-compassion practice is not self-pity or self-indulgence, nor does it let us off the hook if we've done something hurtful or wrong. On the contrary, it provides a kind of holding environment for our pain and humanity, which encourages the motivation to act out of self-love instead of self-dislike. This is because an activated nervous system (when in shame) tends to paralyze us, whereas a downregulated nervous system (when practicing self-kindness and mindfulness) will foster a more action-oriented state of mind.

I like to describe self-compassion practice as cultivating an energy that emanates from our heart-space. It can help to imagine the sensation of tenderness and warmth when cradling an infant (or any preferred adorable species) and offering that same energy to yourself. Try not to get caught up in whether or not you "deserve" self-compassion; keep it simple by choosing to practice it *whenever* you are hurting.

ENCOUNTERING SHAME IN A NEW WAY

So...time to cradle yourself, folks! Next time you recognize you are "in shame," follow the steps of this exercise. For practice, pick a moment when you experienced this painful emotion.

1. Label your state of thought and emotion as *shame* when you catch yourself thinking you are bad or feeling exposed in some way. Say to yourself: *This is shame. I am in shame right now.*

2. Observe the way shame feels in your body and mind. How does your body feel when it is in shame? What does feeling this way make you want to do (for example, yell, hide, punish yourself)?

3. Normalize shame as an emotion experienced by most humans. Shame can make you want to punish yourself. Say to yourself: *I'm feeling shame because I have a natural human desire to feel belonging, acceptance, and love.*

4. Place a hand over your heart (this activates oxytocin, the love hormone, and the care system, which fights the activated nervous system). Say to yourself: *May I know I am worthy. May I know I am lovable. May I know I am human* (Germer and Neff 2020).

5. Share your shame. Shame thrives in the dark, so if you have someone who can hear and see your experience without judgment, speaking up can transform the pain (Brown 2000).

*this is my face
whenever I hear
you talk shit about
yourself, so cut it
out because you're
freakin Awesome*

19. "Nothing good ever lasts"

Although it *is* true that everything is impermanent, this bit of self-talk is what we tell ourselves while we wait for the other shoe to drop. This core belief invites in pessimism and makes us fearful of a letdown or an inevitable rejection. When something good does happen, we're too on edge to soak up the experience. Even when we take a moment to acknowledge some positivity, we still tend to overemphasize any negative aspects. We don't want to get too comfortable, of course. In order to avoid suffering from an outcome that *may or may not occur*, we choose defeatist self-talk, and that will *guarantee* suffering in the present moment. It makes us kind of a bummer.

After the novelty of dating apps wore off in my early twenties, my friends and I slowly became jaded about our love lives. We didn't "date"—we were "meeting up." We scoffed at the idea of getting remotely excited at the prospect of said meetup; we always had nicknames for people we went out with because using their real name would imply a possibility of a relationship, and we couldn't risk believing that it could possibly go anywhere.

Whatever the realm of life, many of us develop the same pessimistic and defeatist attitude toward our careers, friendships, and habit-building endeavors. Our hypervigilance in anticipating the next shitty thing takes away from the ability to take pride or joy in the parts of life we are living.

Some people I've worked with live in a perpetual state of demoralization. It is a familiar and (almost) comforting self-fulfilling prophecy for them. They come to me suffering from depression or anxiety, and for many, the origin story is that they've made certain not to let their guard down for too long. They don't give themselves permission to take in temporary joy, and for that, they suffer the consequences of living in a self-created bubble of discontent.

DELIGHTING WHILE IT LASTS

There's a difference between clinging to a faulty belief system that tells us that nothing good will last (*for us*) and acknowledging that nothing good will last because life is fundamentally ever-changing. In the former, we might live in perpetual fear or helplessness, whereas in the latter we simply learn not to attach ourselves to the prospect that goodness will be a permanent state. This means that we have every expectation that disappointment and letdowns are part of the life package—but we are no longer so afraid.

I remember first learning about the concept of impermanence and feeling immense relief at the idea that I didn't have to hold on to any experience with the expectation that it would be my happiness supply forever. I learned not only to consistently supply my own happiness but also not to miss out on delighting in anything positive for however long it did last. I thanked the moments that made me smile or feel peaceful, if only for a little while.

While suffering is inevitable, it is not permanent either. It takes guts to be vulnerable enough to indulge in good things as they come without constantly bracing for the endings. I do want to recognize the important fact that some of us were conditioned from a young age to wait for the next bad thing to come because getting too comfortable could have genuinely compromised our safety. If that *is* your story, I hope that you are working toward safety and slowly giving yourself permission to savor positive moments.

We can first start to delight in smaller things before working up to the more consequential life stuff. We can put on our favorite song and dance to it before our day begins, noticing the good feeling of moving our body and releasing any stuck energy. We can celebrate the accomplishment for every day we've kept a plant alive. In my work, I remind clients who suffer from panic attacks to celebrate when they go a week without one, to train their mind to believe it can last, and to be confident that they will cope should it not.

NOTICING THE GOOD

Write a sentence about something going well in your life at the moment. Feel free to acknowledge your good health, a new connection you've made, or a new denim jacket you've been wearing every day because it makes you feel good. It can be as simple as *I've been drinking fresh coffee nearly every day out of my favorite mug* or *I'm enjoying having a crush on my hallway neighbor.*

Define and write about a broader and more playful version of "good." For many people, "good things" refer to big-ticket items like being in a relationship or getting an interview for a desired job. Based on our new perspective, "going well" now refers to anything that brings us positive vibes.

Write down and read aloud statements of intention that resonate. They can be more general: *I will celebrate at least one positive thing daily, no matter how long it may last.* Or, more specific: *I will allow myself to feel happy about being pregnant again after having had a miscarriage.*

Practice thanking the existence of a good thing that has indeed found a way to stick around in your life. It can be a particularly resilient pair of socks that you've kept around for years. *Thank you, socks, for continuing to keep my feet cozy, sans holes.*

Remember your resilience. If you're fearful about getting too comfortable, please remind yourself that you will survive, even when the good peters off. Plus, there will be good that comes again.

We have to get creative in a world that finds ways to knock our good vibes. It takes practice to learn how to pay closer attention to positive life experiences while ignoring the dejected voice that tells us they will inevitably end. Soon your self-talk will shift from "Nothing good will last" to "Some good things do last, and I don't need to fear for when they end."

20. "I'm a negative person"

Well, good thing you're halfway through this book—there is hope for you yet! Even if you do have a habit of being Debbie Downer, calling yourself a negative person makes it your entire identity, and I'm pretty sure we put a kibosh on that in an earlier chapter.

Despite years of studying the habits of the mind and making self-talk a priority in my own life, the truth is that no one is immune from the nature of the human mind. However, I'm proud to say that I've learned to flick most negativity away like a fly perched on a slice of watermelon, and although it wasn't an easy road, I'd love for you to experience the benefits of developing a negativity-resilient brain.

So, remember how our brains are wired to anticipate and respond to any potential threat of injury or death? In modern times, the same ancient circuitry now scans its own content and environment for emotional and existential threat. This means that the mind makes sure that we get freaked out over things that literally cannot harm us.

A cognitive distortion called *negative filtering* takes information and causes us to dwell excessively on the parts that make us feel like shit, often while discounting other facts. In essence, we distort the reality of what we hear and process it through a tattered, moldy filtration system and convince ourselves that the gross gunk is the ultimate truth about others, life, and us. The severity of our negative filtering is on a spectrum; some people quickly recover from a moment of self-doubt and others spend nearly every free moment in various states of internalized or externalized negativity such as resentment, bitterness, self-hatred, rage, self-pity, self-reproach, you name it.

Chronically negative folks often become easily irritated or moody and have trouble finding a sense of peace in any given situation. Those who complain or harp on negative aspects of a situation or themselves without having perspective limit their own potential for experiencing positivity and happiness.

Let's look at a simple example: We can all relate to going out for a meal. The company may be great, and the food is really tasty; you might have had a reservation for weeks to a restaurant you had been excited to check out. Overall, you have a really great time—but unfortunately at some point earlier in the night, a friend who was supposed to make it texts you to let you know they need to have a night in. Instead of remembering a pleasant evening connecting with loved ones, perhaps you go home and text everyone who was in attendance how much the late cancellation bothered you and makes you anxious about the state of that friendship. When some of your friends try to validate you or help you shift your perspective, your mind insists on continuing to harp on the one thing that didn't go well.

CHANGING THE FILTER

If you're ready to knock this whole negativity thing on its ass, there are two statements you must start to live and breathe every single day. Repeat after me:

1. It doesn't feel good to focus on the negatives whether aimed at myself or outwardly.

2. I am committed to training my mind to let go of negative self-talk because I want to suffer less.

Living by these truths motivated me to practice daily and genuinely transformed the way I see myself and the world around me. Even when my mind momentarily fixates on worries about our planet or tells me I wasn't a good enough therapist after a session, my reflex now is to be mindful of my negative vibes instead of indulging them.

DITCH NEGATIVITY

You can use the skills you've learned thus far to approach chronic negativity, but here are some more things you can try when negativity rears its ugly head:

1. Note any negativity in the mind. Identify the thought, emotion, and body sensation that arises.

2. Identify where the negativity is being directed and give a brief insight as to why you had the response. Save deeper introspection for a great therapy session. (We love that shit.)

3. When negativity fills your mind, turn your attention to your environment and ask yourself a few questions about what you see (for example, as you notice your impatience while waiting in a long line, you can be curious about where the guy in front of you came from before he got there). Get creative with your sense of wonder and see how much lighter you feel letting go of that negativity filter.

21. "Things are black and white"

Nineties band OTOWN may have said it best with their famous lyrics "'Cause I want it all, or nothing at all," though little did they know they were introducing us to a common self-talk pattern described as *black and white*, or *all-or-nothing*, thinking, which involves viewing everything in extremes. If we see people as all good or all bad, for instance, we will struggle to keep in mind their humanness when they innocently mess up or hurt us. Or, if we make going to the gym a pressure-filled experience, we risk teetering between workout obsession or never going at all.

These cognitive blips are unintended, but they try to protect us from any gray area, which creates a sense of limbo for us in which we may be forced to genuinely confront the most unexplored or uncomfortable chambers of our mind. For many of us, our all-or-nothing mentality and self-talk functioned as a way to delineate clear-cut categories that made sense out of unpredictable situations and created a sense protection against situations that otherwise seemed unclear or unsafe. Here are some familiar areas in which many of us exhibit *dichotomous thinking*—idealization of one thing and complete devaluation of another—and how we can approach the same areas with a gray lens.

TURNING BLACK AND WHITE INTO GRAY

- Looking at certain foods as good or bad * Food is fuel

- Looking at our body as either good or bad * Every single body is different; our worth is not determined by our body

- Thinking of people as either good or bad * No one is all good or all bad; many factors influence a person's personality and behavior

- Accusing people we love of "always" or "never" doing or not doing something when in a fight or angry * They are human and sometimes they do things I don't like, but I love them anyway

- "In" and "out" group ideologies * Humans thrive when they accept one another

- Thinking of ourselves as a failure * We are much more than just our outcomes

- Not getting an A is like getting an F * We aren't defined by arbitrary grading systems

- Dismissing any good qualities any time you confront a flaw * Having a flaw is human nature, and it doesn't mean you don't also have good qualities.

- Interpreting someone being upset with you as them devaluing your identity entirely * Most people can have a negative emotion toward you without attributing it to your entire being

When we think in black and white, we can also have trouble forgiving flaws or imperfect behavior by acknowledging the human condition. All-or-nothing thinking narrows our perspective, making us less psychologically flexible and more defensive.

EMPHASIZING THE GRAY

Though I know black and white are always "in," I'm going to challenge you to make some different fashion choices. We first need to identify this pattern of self-talk as flawed thinking. Once we develop an awareness of the language we use when in an all-or-nothing state, we will get to practice finding the gray. Practicing the following steps will over time help us not get stuck in cycles of idealization and devaluation, which will allow us to hold multiple truths as valid at the same time.

1. Change "always" and "never" into "sometimes." Try to eliminate extreme terms altogether.

2. Remember that a situation can be viewed in more than one way and a problem can be solved in more than one way. Multiple truths need not be mutually exclusive. For example, a partner can lie to you and still be a good person. We can feel we aren't in the mood for something and still choose to do it. We can feel fear and still do what scares us.

3. Note any tension in your body when your mind is in all-or-nothing mode. In this irrational state, we are prone to making impulsive decisions. Take a few minutes to stretch, lie on an acupressure mat, or use a foam roller. Releasing physical tension to downregulate your nervous system will help slow down your reactivity.

4. Listen to more boy bands and practice finding negative self-talk in the lyrics.

22. "I need to be perfect"

Please don't take this personally, but you'll never be perfect—so, let's figure out how to let go of this bit of self-talk once and for all.

Our desire to be seen as perfect may be reflective of having been in a home with high standards or where love and validation were not unconditionally given. Perfection earned us attention or affection, and in other cases, it protected us from punishment or rejection. Some of us perfectionists chase the feeling of being in control, believing that "exactly right" equates to "safe and predictable."

Whatever the origin of the belief system, every human craves feeling valued. This can yield a constant sense that something's missing in us, propelling us to try to fill that void. When we don't feel as though we're enough of something—smart enough, thin enough, interesting enough—we strive to compensate in order to prove ourselves worthy of belonging and acceptance.

What sucks is that we are set up to fail—perfection is unattainable. To describe something as "perfect" implies it has no flaws or defects. When it comes to people, this is already impossible because everyone is inherently flawed, as this is the nature of being human. What's more, perfection is entirely subjective, making it impossible to reach because the goalposts always move. When our standards of perfection aren't met, overly critical self-talk inevitably follows, often determining our self-esteem and worth.

I suppose there are rare exceptions. One time I was waxing poetic with a client with deep self-loathing, trying to convince her of the humanity of imperfection. "No one will ever get there," I maintained.

She looked at me and genuinely asked, "What about Beyoncé? You're telling me that she isn't perfect?"

Welp. She had me there.

ACCEPTING YOUR IMPERFECT SELF

For the rest of us mere mortals, it can be painful to confront that we may never achieve perfection in an effort to overtake the little voice that says, "not good enough." Instead, we find comfort in avoidance. I procrastinated writing because I knew I had a tendency to get stuck for hours, plagued by a compulsive need to fix one sentence until it felt "perfect." I was scared that unless I provided the "perfect writing," "perfect examples," and "perfectly unique exercises," then I would be seen as an impostor who wrote yet another generic self-help book.

Letting up on our perfectionistic tendencies means letting go of the control we *think* we have over how others will perceive us or our behaviors. We can check ourselves by doing some introspective self-talk: *Do I* need *to be perfect to be lovable and worthy?* or *Is there someone who finds me totally acceptable despite my imperfection?* or *Isn't it good enough if this book helps even just one person?*

Letting go of safety-zone behaviors is hard, so I'm going to have to get bossy: you have no choice but to start accepting yourself exactly as you are. Instead of perpetuating the cycle of feeling like we've failed or will never be good enough, I implore us to radically alter our philosophy by choosing to know that our best at any given moment *is* enough. Technically, however we behaved or handled life in a given moment *was* our best—there is no way to go back in time. We must learn to unconditionally accept our reality and to do so radically—that is, without judgment, realizing things for what they are, not what we want them to be.

LEARNING TO BE GOOD ENOUGH

Say it with me: "I accept that perfection is unattainable." Relaxing your facial muscles and your body as you practice acceptance statements can help dissolve any resistance. Repeat slowly a few times before you engage in some mindful self-reflection. As always, I encourage doing this exercise on paper!

> What does "perfect" mean to you? What does it look like when you've achieved perfection?
>
> What do you fear about not being perfect?
>
> Whose definition of perfection do you try to live by? Why?
>
> Fill in the blank (choose as many words as you like): I am not _____ enough.
>
> Write about more neutral and positive ways to look at your imperfections.
>
> What will change for the better when you let go of your need to be perfect?
>
> What are some more self-compassionate ways you can talk to yourself when you're feeling like you aren't perfect enough?

Ask yourself, "Would I tell my younger self that they needed to be perfect for me to love and value them?"

Finish by reading the following statements. Write them down on a piece of paper that you can stick on your mirror or somewhere you'll see them every day. Practice reading them daily so they can become your new truth.

I accept that I am imperfect.

I am imperfect, and that's okay.

I am good enough. "Good enough" is enough.

I accept Beyoncé might be the one exception to the rule.

23. "Other people are better than me"

Let's face it: comparison is an insidious game that we will always lose.

Social pressures, changing milestone markers, and the perpetual window into our peers' lives thanks to technology have warped our realities and worsened self-perceptions. We tend to place the worst version of ourselves next to the *perceived* best version of whatever we're fixated on. We see a picture on social media and make judgments about our enoughness, coolness, goals we haven't yet achieved, or how we feel about our bodies—the options for comparison are infinite. The belief in our inadequacy poisons our self-image.

How much time would you guess you've spent suffering, wanting aspects of *others'* lives while neglecting your own? We idealize lifestyles and personas, although we don't have all the facts about other people's realities. We will always find someone who has something we don't, but the issue arises when we allow comparison to devalue us via heavy-duty shit-talking. Comparison keeps us stuck by causing our brain to hyperfocus on what we don't like about ourselves and our life. We say shit to ourselves like:

I wish things came that easily to me—they don't even have to try.

I'll never make as much money as they do.

I lack their grit and commitment.

It sucks to always be the single one.

I should already have my shit together like others my age.

If I hadn't been so lazy, I would have been successful sooner.

If I had their body, dating would be easier.

I wish I had a group of close friends like they do.

I'm sure they always have plans.

I don't have the skills they do to get where I want to in life.

I'll never be as successful as they are.

I'm jealous of their lifestyle/wealth/body.

I can promise you that spending precious life energy dwelling on any version of these beliefs will not inspire you to be a better version of yourself. On the contrary, the resulting low self-esteem and devaluing self-talk are paralyzing and prevent us from carving our own path.

Nurture *your* growth. The antidote to demoralizing comparison is focusing on what you genuinely wish to nurture in yourself, identifying the intrinsic values that make you feel true to yourself, and creating a plan to work toward self-actualization.

The time you spend looking over at someone else's life will slowly drain your life's supply. If we choose to sow our own seeds and tend to our garden, instead of bitterly staring over at the neighbor's *perfect* veggie crops every year, we will see our own greenery flourish and celebrate it, too.

Follow your own logic. You torture yourself with comparisons, but logically, if you want something badly, the only way to satisfy the wanting is to go out and get it for yourself. Comparative self-talk results in time spent wishing, rather than taking action.

Learn to shift perspective. If someone has a quality you deeply value or a skill you wish you'd learned, take steps toward supporting your growth in that direction. If you've assessed that it's realistic to achieve what you are inspired by, then do what it takes to get there.

Develop an accurate analysis of yourself. Describe your skills, qualities, place in your life, and career without infusing the descriptions with your opinion or disillusionment. If you can't be objective, use your "phone a friend" lifeline and talk to someone who can be truthful with you without judgment—like a fantastically smart therapist. Know of any?

Notice your narrative. Notice any time you start writing a story without all the evidence. For example, you see an influencer who always takes the "perfect selfie." With your "I'm less than" blinders up, your story omits that they take nearly one thousand photos to find one that they can show off to the public.

Become curious about your comparison. Are you noticing someone's success in a field you're not even interested in? Are you jealous of a romantic relationship that you've idealized? Answer honestly and you may realize you have no need to compare yourself in the first place.

Drop the fixation. Write down productive ways to nurture your authentic self. Remember that self-growth is more likely to be positive and long-lasting when it comes from self-love rather than comparisons to others.

Cultivate sympathetic joy. Sympathetic joy is the practice of delighting in someone's well-being, successes, and happiness. It is a brilliant and effective way to vanquish envy and cultivate more positive emotions. Take a moment to softly smile to yourself and celebrate another's happiness. Say gently to yourself: *Their happiness does not mean less happiness left for me. Their success does not mean there is less success left for me.* Everyone can have a piece of the pie.

24. "I'm always assuming"

Our thinking mind—let's call her Lou—is deeply flawed and wreaks unnecessary havoc. We don't judge her for it because she does the best she can considering the amount of unwanted input she receives over her lifetime. Okay, so she overdoes it a *bit* sometimes—like when she jumps to conclusions without having all the facts straight. Sometimes, she sets us up to make hasty, inaccurate evaluations of people's intentions and thoughts, for example. Yet, we give her a lot of power to influence our mood and perception. Here are ways in which Lou (*your* thinking mind) flaunts her flaw:

Fortune telling: Lou freaks you out about an inevitably shitty future outcome, acting as if she has a crystal ball. Lou likes to convince you that past struggle is always indicative of similar future suffering.

Mind reading: Lou makes you believe you know way more about the content of someone's mind than you actually have access to. When I start telling a story, for example, Lou makes me anxious that my story isn't interesting or that I'm talking too much.

Extreme extrapolation: Lou takes a small piece of information, overdramatizes it, and makes you anxious as fuck. Like when you innocently missed a therapy appointment and spent a week guilt-tripping yourself because you were sure your therapist was disappointed. (It happens a lot more than you think.)

Overgeneralization: Lou uses a stored memory or a factual experience and then generalizes it to an unrealistic or unreasonable degree. Imagine a scenario where you rarely match with anyone you've liked on a dating app. Jaded ol' Lou then claims "you'll never meet anyone."

Labeling: Lou relies on our beliefs to label characteristics within ourselves and those around us. Unfortunately, this can have some pretty negative consequences since we tend to create identities around labels. For example, when Lou tells you that lazy people are failures, any time you behave lazily, you may label yourself as a failure.

STICK TO THE FACTS

Getting to know Lou is an easier and sillier way for us to understand that we *aren't* our mind. However, we can't blame it all on her—we're still accountable for how we respond to her by transforming our self-talk and our behaviors. Perhaps Lou gets you to believe that a boss won't be cool with your request for time off just because they aren't responding quickly enough—your anxiety goes through the roof. You end up wishing you didn't ask for the vacation you desperately need. It's then *your* responsibility to remind yourself of the various plausible reasons for their nonresponse instead of assuming your boss is annoyed with you for asking. You can also own the fact that you work hard and that asking for time off is absolutely reasonable in a job environment.

ADDRESSING LOU'S CONCLUSION-JUMPING TENDENCIES

Put down the crystal ball: Think of a typical scenario where you predict your "poor" outcome based on past experiences. Explore the aspects of the situation that you may have some control over. What can you do to empower yourself to potentially influence a different outcome?

Give up telepathy: Remember how minds are too busy indulging in their own Lou chatter to give you all that much thought (no offense)? Write about a situation where you were wrong or didn't have enough information about what you assumed someone was thinking. What were the consequences?

Don't make mountains out of molehills: Most times, if you smell smoke, it's not indicative of a fire. Reflect on what kind of events you tend to blow out of proportion and how it impacts your subsequent behavior.

Don't paint with broad strokes: During the pandemic, many people who had to apply for new jobs either weren't hearing back or weren't making it past an interview round. All too soon, they were convinced they'd *never* get a job, which demoralized them and led them to stop applying. Write about a time when your generalizing self-talk negatively affected an outcome.

Let go of labels: Dig deeper by exploring how you have used labeling in a way that erroneously assumed the expected behavior of an individual or group. How have labels affected you?

25. "I don't want to feel this way"

Fair enough—feeling bad, feels...*bad*—but there's a reason that's the case.

Before we develop the language to describe our inner world, we experience sensations thanks to hormones like oxytocin (#love) and cortisol (#stress) and neurotransmitters like dopamine (#happiness). This physical and physiological experience of emotions becomes our first layer of understanding that they can be distinguished as "good" or "bad"—though of course without language, our definition is not at all nuanced.

Simultaneously, our caregivers model their responses to our emotional expression using body language, facial expressions, tone, behavior, and language. If, for example, every time we cried our parent became overwhelmed and anxious, we learned that crying—and the emotion behind it perhaps—was something potentially intolerable. We came to realize that certain emotions were reinforced, while others were discouraged (or devalued, invalidated, and shamed). So, instead of viewing them as normal phenomena that came with the territory of being a human, we were taught to judge (or dislike, or avoid, or resist) them.

So if emotions are in fact *fundamentally* harmless events, we can conclude that our response—"not liking" and "not wanting" —to them is what signals to our brain that these feelings are an unwanted, negative experience. If we can transform our relationship to emotional pain by no longer viewing the rising and falling of difficult emotions as something to be fearful or avoidant of, we can start to accept whatever feeling arises instead of judging it.

OBSERVING YOUR MIND

If you already feel how you feel, what's the sense in judging the experience? If you don't want to feel some kind of way, then you may have to take action to change it. Learning how to be an observer of your inner experience takes practice, and you can start with this exercise!

1. Set an intention to practice catching yourself any time you're resisting a particular emotion or set of thoughts. Resistance looks like wishing for reality to be anything other than it is. When you set an intention, you're saying to yourself that you deeply value whatever it is you want to do, and that you intend to commit to it.

2. Practice nonjudgment. Consciously acknowledge that a thought you have is neither good nor bad; it's just a thought. Like an owl perched on a high branch, simply observe the flow of thinking, feeling, sensing from up high. With nonjudgment, there is no pressure to do anything about your experience because you are no longer telling your nervous system that it is *bad*.

3. Learn to think of thoughts as mere phenomena in the brain—like electricity. For example, when you realize you've been ruminating on how far behind you are compared to your peers, note any distress that arises from the thoughts. This distress is all your mind-made, self-wreaking havoc.

4. Practice this over and over again for the rest of your life.

26. "Life is unfair"

Scientists have found that we are evolutionarily hardwired to recognize fairness, and when we experience or witness unfairness, our amygdala acts up, followed closely by emotions like anxiety or frustration. Our familiarity with unfairness starts early, often when we experience minor woes. Maybe we were forced to share our sandbox shovel or take turns on the swing—before long, there's a whimper, a quivering lip, and tiny hands made into fists; we're convinced the other kid had a much longer turn than we did and it just doesn't *feel* fair. If I were a parent, I might turn to this child and say, "Well, darling, this is a good time for an important lesson about life and the expectation of fairness…"

As teens, we experience getting grounded for *who-cares-what* because it made us miss a sleepover and "It's, like, so unfair!" Then as we grow up, we begin to realize that even the best relationships come with some vintage designer emotional baggage, and soon it is during conflict when we struggle to accept an unfair imbalance of responsibilities or use tit-for-tat methods to point out our partner's wrongdoings.

Unfairness crops up everywhere like a stubborn weed. People we love don't love us back, we work jobs that don't pay us enough, people who lack empathy get ahead in life, others are born with talents we couldn't dream of cultivating, we're single while everyone else seems to have someone, and we struggle to catch a break while our friends seem to float through life without a stumble. The list is endless, and it doesn't even include the egregious injustices that systemically happen in our country and all over the world, outside the tunnel vision of our daily lives.

So, I kindly ask that you don't shoot the messenger when I say…life *isn't* fucking fair.

I spend my days validating the painful emotions that come up for people who believe life has screwed them. It *totally* sucks, especially because there are times when we've been genuinely wronged. As humans, we crave to address the wrongdoing, or we ruminate on the fact that it's happened to us in the first place.

However, the self-talk that causes us the most suffering uses the concept of fairness to avoid taking responsibility for aspects of our life we don't like, many of which are in some way a result of our doing or nondoing. Have you ever thought about the unfairness of others' strengths and success? Or complained about how a job didn't pay you enough even though you went above and beyond? Have you ever thought *I just need one thing to go my way for once?*

Maybe it's difficult to admit that instead of being paralyzed by comparison or fear, we could have taken that time to develop a skill or get up the courage to ask for a raise. Instead of confronting something about ourselves we don't like, we blame it away or victimize ourselves. Unfortunately, ruminating on unfairness is not only a waste of your precious energy but it also won't change any outcomes.

REINTERPRETING FAIRNESS

Unfairness is a bitter pill to swallow, so I recommend chasing it with a tasty liquid. I find that acceptance with a splash of accountability on the rocks typically does the trick.

First, let's note that there are situations we associate with fairness that are *within our control* and situations that are *out of our control*. Regardless of our perceived or actual level of control, we are not powerless. We can choose how we integrate fairness into our everyday behaviors and into our interactions with others. More importantly, we have a choice as to how we respond to the perceived wrongs we experience and observe.

It rains on people's wedding days and nonsmokers get lung cancer. Bad shit happens to innocent people while assholes get a slap on the wrist. It's important to note that when it comes to things out of our control, we often fail to recognize that what's actually present is not perceived unfairness but a sense of *entitlement*. We believe people or the universe owe us something—we want to be recognized for our good deeds and accomplishments. We want the fair exchange we feel we deserve. We want life to chill instead of act up.

But life doesn't give a shit about your happiness and the universe doesn't have a hidden agenda. Pema Chödrön says, "As human beings, not only do we seek resolution, but we also feel that we deserve resolution. However, not only do we not deserve resolution, we suffer from resolution" (Chödrön 2000, 54). Ruminating on life's unfair moments and behaving like victims of occurrences beyond our control—all while feeling owed a different outcome—keeps us paralyzed in the past and fosters a sense of powerlessness. Remember from past chapters that when we resist accepting reality, we suffer. When we accept it, there is freedom. In essence, our peace lies in the quality of our response to perceived unfairness.

THE SEVEN A'S OF TRANSFORMING UNFAIRNESS

Acknowledge all the ways you perceive life has been unfair, either to you or to others. Do your best not to judge your perception; simply acknowledge it.

Allow for any difficult emotion like anger or grief to freely arise, and pause every so often to notice how your body is feeling. We aren't trying to make any tough emotional experience go away—we are making room for these very normal emotional by-products of feeling wronged or witnessing injustice. Eventually, this practice will reduce our emotional reactivity so that we can respond in productive and mindful ways.

Ask yourself, *Did I have any control over this experience?* Identify whether you played any role in perpetuating or creating an unfair experience, or if life's randomness or others' actions are generating it.

Accept the reality that life is unfair and full of random luck that affects all of humanity.

Adjust your expectations. Once you know not to expect fairness, you won't have to suffer from the outcomes that you would otherwise feel wronged by.

Adapt to a new philosophy. Remind yourself that you *don't* have any control over unfairness except for your response, which will ultimately determine how much more suffering you're piling on.

Act wisely. Instead of disempowering yourself by perpetuating narratives in which you've been slighted, you now know that you can choose how long you grieve, mope, stay angry, act resentful, or refuse to accept an outcome of something.

27. "I take things too personally"

I sincerely hope you haven't taken the sass strewn about these pages too personally. If you have taken it personally, I want to reassure you that it's not *you*—it's...your brain.

Although that sounds like a creative version of a clichéd breakup line, it's actually an important reminder that our brains are wired to ensure that we are generally at the center of our own mental universe. Our mind is always scanning the environment for danger—and in this case, it's prepared to respond to any perceived threats to our ego (sense of self or conditioned identity). Unfortunately, since our fear center did not adaptively evolve to cope with modern-day psychological stressors, much of our inner voice remains rooted in unconscious defense mechanisms.

There's no need to give yourself a hard time about it—personalization is an über-common defensive reflex aimed at protecting our vulnerable psyche. It can develop as a result of pervasive outside criticism or devaluing, when we learn that there are conditions we must meet in order to be accepted or loved (for example, by caregivers, peers, etc.). Our minds enter a state of fear when we perceive that we are not meeting someone's criteria for worthiness of belonging—this fear makes us reactive in order to defend ourselves against whatever we believe threatens our self-image.

Each of us has insecurities that influence what we tend to personalize. I get self-conscious about how passionately I speak. I'm not exactly known for my brevity. Growing up, there were constant negative reactions to my too-muchness and, for years, if someone casually mentioned my storytelling being long or playfully joked about how I talked a lot, my face got hot and I behaved in a reactive or sarcastic way.

Even though most comments were innocuous, I never responded calmly to perceived devaluation, invalidation, misunderstanding, or rejection. And although it was important for me to work on my defensiveness, I didn't need to pile on the judgment that I was simply too sensitive, thereby invalidating my very real experience.

LEARN HOW NOT TO MAKE IT ABOUT YOU

The trouble with taking everything to heart is that we create more suffering for ourselves even when most people do not intend to wound us. Other people's behavior is *never* about us. What humans say is by default a projection of their own reality, filtered through the lens of their own discomforts, fears, wants, values, and needs. If you choose to live by this truth, you can begin to let go of any reflex to personalize another's behavior.

Here are some of the consequences of personalization and how you might respond:

Overidentification with negative thoughts, emotions, and other people's opinions of you as undeniable reflections of a fixed identity * Cultivate mindful awareness to maintain a sense of objectivity; Don't extrapolate an egregious character flaw from a mistake or isolated behavior

Reflexive or unconscious defensive reactions where we try to rationalize, justify, deny, gaslight, or project blame * Build the self-awareness to consider the facts and practice self-compassion toward your flawed self

Guilt-tripping and ruminating on ways something must have been our fault or due to flaws * Take accountability in a situation with an undesirable outcome and make efforts to work on any parts of yourself that would benefit from change

Feelings of responsibility for the emotional and behavioral responses of other people * Understand that each human is responsible for their own actions and emotional well-being; recognize that many factors affect someone's mood state or reaction

Low self-esteem/self-worth due to the self-blame and belief that life struggles and disappointments are a character failing * Practice self-compassion to acknowledge the humanness of any challenging experience or discouraging outcome

A fear of being disliked and of others noticing flaws/an inability to be present in social situations due to obsessive thinking and worry about how we may appear * Normalize that everyone worries or wonders what others think of them; strengthen your core worth so that you are not as rattled by the idea that someone might not like you; know that every single human is deeply flawed

Inability to take constructive criticism without overreacting or jumping to conclusions; feeling hurt very easily and growing even more fearful of judgment * Understand the intention behind constructive criticism and know that most people don't have a hidden agenda to devalue us; choose to be excited to learn and be better in all aspects of life, and welcome constructive feedback

Misattributing certain negative qualities to people if we read them wrong; having miscommunications and misunderstandings in relationships and friendships that can lead to greater conflict * Learn how to ask people what they really mean instead of personalizing through our own negative filter and jumping to conclusions

28

"I feel responsible for other people"

Here is a little secret: therapists make a living thanks to our unresolved savior complexes.

Feeling responsible for others is often a consequence of growing up in a home where a parent's dysregulated, reactive, dismissive, or unpredictable emotionality ruled the day. When a parent is incapable of providing emotional safety or regulation, a child is forced to step into the parental role in order to mitigate some of the chaos. They also may learn to hide their own struggles because they know they cannot count on the adults in the home.

It is important to distinguish "feeling responsible" from "choosing to be responsible." Due to our tendency to overidentify with an emotional state, it is much easier to fall into this self-talk trap when we get caught up in the *feeling* or *pressure* of needing to take care of someone's emotional or mental well-being—especially if there is some level of guilting or manipulation involved. We begin to fear what will happen if we don't.

However, even with a compelling request for our support, we always have the agency to opt out. If we continue to convince ourselves that we are responsible for others' emotional states, we risk becoming people-pleasers, overaccommodators, and neglecters of our own needs and boundaries.

HOLD OTHERS AND OURSELVES ACCOUNTABLE

Life is hard enough without us taking on the feelings of others, believing we're liable for another's bad mood, or thinking we're powerful enough to play a deciding factor in someone's successes or failures. It is not realistic nor sustainable to believe and act as though we hold the power to make people feel or behave some kind of way.

Any phrase beginning with "you made me" is used to accuse someone of *causing* emotional and behavioral reactivity in us. It enables our belief that people can *make* us do and feel things that we have absolutely no control over when, in reality, we can learn how to have healthier emotional responses and hold ourselves accountable instead of feeling powerless to the whims of our emotional selves.

HOW TO JUST BE RESPONSIBLE FOR YOURSELF

1. Recognize that adults have agency over their own lives. They are ultimately the ones making the choices that will lead to their level of life satisfaction.

2. Let go of the control you think you have or think you want in order to keep others' chaos at bay.

3. Don't apologize when you have no evidence of wrongdoing. Oftentimes, I will run over time with a patient because I decide to pursue a recently opened can of worms too close to an end of a session. I continue asking the questions, and then when they realize the time, they tend to say, "Oh, I'm so sorry, I made you late," to which I always reply, "Hey, I made a *choice* to stay and keep talking."

4. Acknowledge the choice *you* have in how *you* respond both emotionally and behaviorally to others' turmoil or discontent. Would you want other people to think they are the ones who hold the key to your ability to cope with life?

5. Think about the various factors that genuinely influence a person's well-being: their upbringing, the stress at work that day, their trauma history. This will allow you to separate from how you erroneously believe you are impacting them.

6. Check your boundaries. Are you feeling responsible because you're interacting with someone who doesn't respect emotional boundaries or whose erratic emotionality makes you walk on eggshells? Taking on someone else's emotions often means that the lines between your feelings and their feelings are blurring.

7. When you start to feel guilty for thinking you're the cause of someone's negative experience, develop a mantra you can repeat to yourself that sounds like, "I am not responsible for this person's struggles and discontents in life. They have the ability to be accountable, just like I do."

PRO TIP: Understand the difference between empathy and compassion when engaging with others. Empathy involves putting ourselves in someone's shoes and often acutely coexperiencing their pain. Compassion involves acknowledging someone's suffering and feeling care or concern for someone in their distress. While empathy is crucial for the understanding of how others feel, feeling intense emotions that aren't even ours will exhaust us. Shifting from empathy to compassion gives us that extra space that we need to not become fatigued or stay feeling responsible. We can practice being present while regulating our own nervous system, which will allow us to act from a place of understanding and warmth without taxing all of our emotional resources.

29

"This feels like it will last forever"

"I feel like this will never end" thought every person who's experienced any kind of suffering.

I remember the immense heartache when my boyfriend and I broke up after five years. At eighteen, I was convinced we were going to get married. Cut to five years later and I was leaving our Boston home, sobbing uncontrollably, and terrified that I would never recover after having royally fucked up my best chance at happiness. I really believed I would never meet someone like him again and live with the pain of regret forever. Three months later, I was one of the first millennials swiping right on Tinder Beta.

Emotional pain can distort our sense of time, creating an illusion that we will have to endure the aching and the mental anguish for eternity. Additionally, with our fight-or-flight kicked into gear, we get tunnel vision, and it becomes nearly impossible to see possibility outside of our current state of inner turmoil. Remember that when our nervous system kicks in, our prefrontal cortex—the part of the brain responsible for conscious decision making, long-term planning, and self-control—kind of shuts off (great timing, right?). Especially for those of us who struggle with regulating emotions and moods, our experience of an unpleasant emotion magnifies in intensity and perceived duration.

Do you remember an embarrassing moment in high school? An unexpected breakup with someone you cared about? A betrayal? Each of us has had moments where we were so wrapped up in a state of hurt that being mindful was out of the question and before us lay a winding path of inevitable misery. Due to humans' attachment to the concept of permanence, our self-talk reflects a doom-and-gloom attitude that amplifies our ruminations and thought-spiraling.

Let's refer back to the very first chapter where we were convinced we couldn't or wouldn't change...

EVERYTHING IS IMPERMANENT

There are plenty of things we *wish* would never change that inevitably do before our eyes. My darling puppy and kitten are growing at astonishing rates, and I whine about it almost every day. However, when it comes to the experiences that cause us the kind of suffering that we wish would end immediately, like heartbreak, identity crises, depressive episodes, and some presidential campaigns, somehow these feel like they will last forever. To amplify the discomfort, life seems to flaunt its uncertain ways, and we suffer from the fear that comes with not knowing, making it that much more difficult to remember that everything eventually goes away.

Nearly two trillion cells divide in a human body every day, which means that nothing—not bad weather, suffering of any kind, our bodies, nor life itself—lasts forever. When we lean into this truth about impermanence, we begin to let go of the fears we have of tolerating future pain. We know it will not last.

Know with all your heart and all your might that it will not last.

30. "I'm the only one who struggles like this"

Well, I sure hope that's not the case—otherwise, I'll only manage to sell one of these books...

Sometimes painful experiences are so overpowering, strange, or shameful that we feel isolated in our experience of them. It can feel as though no one else could possibly be as flawed as we are, think the same strange things that we do, or behave as selfishly as we can. We may believe that everyone else is somehow doing life "more right" than we are.

I can usually tell someone is feeling isolated in their pain when they talk about how "bad" they are. Then, right as I attempt to reassure them or challenge their belief system, they lean in, lower their voice and say, "No, Katie, you don't *understand*. I'm a *garbage human*." Or something to that effect.

Don't get me wrong: I'm sure you're pretty freaking awesome. That being said, remember that this book wasn't written *just* for you, so you can safely assume there are at least a handful of others in whatever boat you're in. Remember the billions of people also on the planet? It's simply illogical that there isn't at least one other human with whom you share even the darkest or weirdest of thoughts.

You are *never* alone in the way your mind functions or what it comes up with. Trust me. And with eight billion people living on this earth, in the shocking case that you *are* the *only* one...then I congratulate you on a Guinness World Record–level feat.

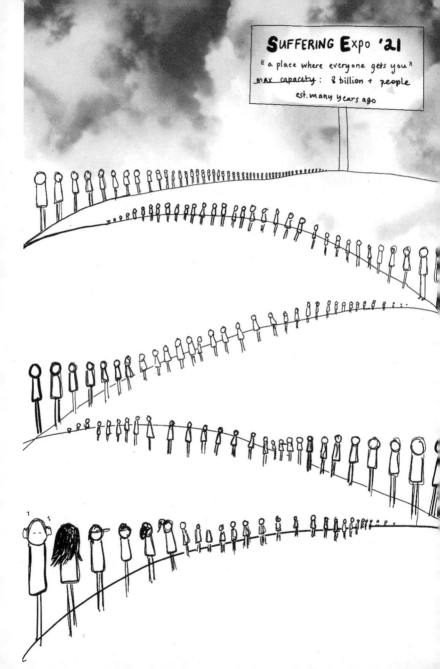

31. "I'm afraid of what they'll think of me"

For the record, I've been a little nervous about what you've been thinking of me while reading this book. This type of self-talk happens to the best of us.

Just under the giving-a-shit-about-what-people-think-of-us theme alone, there is an infinite number of combinations of negative, fear-based, and self-critical statements and thoughts. We are afraid of what people will think about how we look, what we say and how we say it, our personality, and our flaws if we don't hide them well enough. Even for those of us who are lucky enough or have worked hard enough to maintain a good self-esteem when it comes to our social self, it is still difficult to fully eliminate a baseline fear of being rejected or "found out" in some way.

Many of us have an amplified fear of how we are perceived thanks to well-conditioned core beliefs (see chapter 15) that we are unlikeable or unacceptable. This harsh self-talk serves to remind us that we need to be extra careful when it comes to doing things that will ensure our belonging. The fear-based mindset in interpersonal interactions can turn us into people-pleasers, chronic overapologizers, self-guilt-trippers, accommodators, and yes-folk.

Ultimately, as long as we care too much about what people think of us, we will continue to tell ourselves some version of all forty statements in this book—and that's *just* in reference to protecting ourselves against the pain of potential social rejection.

We desire to experience a sense of validation from a group, so some of us may even behave in inauthentic ways, believing that we need to act a certain way to compensate for what we fear we lack. My very best friend tells the story of how we met in our middle school choir. Or more accurately, how she noticed my (innocent) attention-seeking ways of being a loud, try-hard, class clown. Choir clown in this case. "I thought you were annoying at first," she tells me every time.

I *know* I was obnoxious because my validation-seeking behaviors ranged from comical to cringeworthy. Perhaps at that age I wasn't explicitly worrying about what other kids were thinking about me, but I certainly behaved in ways that implied my desperate desire to feel a sense of belonging. I think I tried so hard because somewhere in my core there was an unconscious sense that I needed to be extra to cover up a fundamental deficiency. We've been best friends for over eighteen years, so ultimately this is a story of triumph.

DEVELOPING RESILIENCE

Growing up, we observed and participated in social experiences where we learned what to do and what not to do in order to be liked. We care about what people think of us because we had higher evolutionary chances of survival when we were in a group, making respect and trust from humans vital. We learned what qualities were deemed the most worthy of belonging—apparently, musical theater skills don't always help us fit in, but that's the cool kids' loss. Many factors influence who gets to belong, including stages of development, current events, cultural and familial values, and the environment, to name a few.

Given all the many influencing factors, we need to develop a way to cope with the possibility of being judged, no matter the situation. Dr. Brené Brown (shame expert and idol) developed a model that helps us do just that called *shame resilience theory* (Brown 2007).

Based on her research, Dr. Brown concludes that shame needs to be understood and brought to light by speaking about it before shame can begin to loosen its grip. Dr. Brown also emphasizes the ways in which folks high in courage, compassion, and connection are more inoculated against experiencing shame, suggesting that if we work to develop those qualities, we too could see the epic benefits (Brown 2007).

We are much less likely to place a high value or meaning on to what others think when we aren't shaky about who we are. When we know, work on, and accept ourselves, we can grow into our most authentic self—and we will not allow others' opinions to define any part of our identity.

To get there, we must have handy the practice of self-compassion and empathy because it allows us to have the courage to be vulnerable even at the risk of being misunderstood, devalued, or rejected. People who are very empathic are also highly resilient to shame (Brown 2007). They know what shame sounds like, looks like, and feels like, and they understand what can trigger it in themselves and others. They also have empathy for the pain of shame, which typically results in acting toward others in kind, less judgmental ways to help others experience the positive feeling of connection.

SHUTTING OUT SHAME

Anytime you start to feel shame, you can practice the following exercise. For now, visualize a moment where you remember worrying about what people were thinking of you—maybe after you said or did something you worried would not be accepted. Then practice going through the following steps:

1. Label it as *shame* when you catch yourself thinking that you are annoying, unlikeable, unworthy, etc. Say to yourself: *Oh! That's shame!* or *Woah! There's shame again!*

2. Soften your body and take a deep breath. Say to yourself: *I'm feeling shame because I have a normal human desire to feel belonging, acceptance, and love.*

3. Close your eyes and picture the faces of people closest to you, as well as strangers all over the world. Knowing that they all experience shame, say to yourself:

   Wow, I know that nearly every human feels this painful emotion. It's part of our human experience. I'm not alone in that.

4. Begin to nonjudgmentally observe, much like a scientist would, the way shame feels in your body. See how its physicality changes over time.

5. Use gentle or firm touch to offer yourself comfort. Cup your face in your hands or give yourself a tight hug.

6. Shame typically makes us want to fight (anger/resentment), flee (ruminate), or freeze (hide out). Think of what the shame is making you *want* to do. Now think of something that is the complete *opposite*. For example, if you just had a fight with your family because they told you that you gained too much weight, and it makes you want to unfollow all of them on Instagram, can you practice number five, and then check in with your impulse? (Krimer 2020)

32. "I always _____ / I never _____"

Let's fill in the blanks. What comes to your mind when you read these prompts aloud to yourself? What is it that you think you *always* are or *always* do? What is it you're convinced you *never* are or *never* do?

I'll go first. I *always* use the words "always" and "never" when in a conflict with my partner. The fight is usually over something silly that I tell him he *never* does, like put in a new toilet paper roll (upon reflection, this is likely untrue—jury's still out).

"Always" and "never" are subsets of the black-and-white thinking mentality, which as we know, limits our perspective of ourselves, others, and the world. Sometimes it is easier to sum something up with a catchall term; however, if our use of "always" or "never" gives an inaccurate reflection of our capabilities or isn't representative of the evidence, then we want to become more mindful of when they crop up in our daily conversations.

SPEAKING LESS CATEGORICALLY

You might be happy to know there's no long-winded explanation or exercise for this one because it has a pretty simple solution: in daily conversation and self-talk, practice eliminating these words unless you are exaggerating for effect or if they are numerically accurate (always = every single time; never = zero times).

For example, I can tell you that I have *never* skydived. However, saying "I will never skydive" changes the meaning to imply that I have already made a categorical decision in my mind. Hey, if it's true, it's true. (But generally, I try my best not to use "never" or "always" when describing or promising an uncertain future... because we simply just don't know.) Otherwise, replace with words like *sometimes, rarely, nearly, much of the time,* etc. for a little more wiggle room.

Practice by poking holes in these examples:

I always know what people are thinking.

I never invalidate anyone's emotions.

I am always there for everyone else.

I will never be able to change.

33. "I'm not where I should be in life by now"

This line of self-talk is a neat combo of *shoulding* yourself (see #11), a sprinkle of comparing yourself to others (see #23), and a smattering of some of the other shitty inner commentary I've covered thus far. When we say shit like this, we're implying that there are milestones in life we must achieve by a certain time in order to succeed or to unlock further stages of life happiness. Telling ourselves that we aren't where we want to be in life is an effective way to demoralize ourselves and pummel any remaining self-esteem.

If you haven't caught on, this is generally what *all* negative self-talk successfully accomplishes: when you talk shit, you're more likely to feel like shit, which makes you more likely to believe you're a piece of shit—you know, that whole thing.

The majority of folks I see are between the ages of twenty and thirty-five, so it makes sense why I hear about made-up or socially conditioned timelines nearly every day, all day. Given all the milestones we're "meant" to hit during that fifteen-year span, there's a whole lotta self-judgment that gets flung around if you're "behind." That said, older adults commonly talk about milestones they should have met some time ago, which is bound to propagate regret, and keep them stuck in the past. There are many versions of this statement and some of them sound like...

- I should have chosen a more useful major.

- Everyone else knows what their purpose is.

- I should have figured out my career passion by now.

- Others my age have their shit together.

- I should be making more money by now.

- I can't believe I'm still at an entry-level job.

- I should have had a long-term relationship already.

- I wanted to be married by now.

Take a pause and muse upon your typical self-talk about ways in which you believe you're behind. Note how it makes you feel.

ACCEPT YOUR OWN TIMELINE

Look, I can definitely commiserate with you on this topic. For a long time, I had a nagging and anxiety-provoking thought that I absolutely had to be a young mother in order to have a fulfilling relationship with my child. Now childless at thirty-one, I am grateful for my timeline because it allowed me to have many of my own adventures.

Still, I acutely know the sensation of looking over at peers and deciding that you're bad or flawed because you aren't where they are. But if you Google "life's timeline," you will read about objectively successful people whose lives are all over the map. Morgan Freeman's big break happened when he was fifty!

The truth is the things we haven't done—they're in the past. The things we've yet to do—they're in the future. While the behaviors we choose on our path have some influence, there are endless external factors of life that unfold however they feel like it.

Next time you're giving yourself a hard time about not being where you want to be in life, give yourself these reminders:

1. The idea that there is an age limit to do most things is a made-up construct. Everyone's life path is unique, and no amount of comparison will change it.

2. I would never say to someone else that they aren't where they "should" be, so I won't say it to myself.

3. I *accept* the things I haven't done in my life up until this point because I know I cannot change the past.

4. My fixation on a timeline is related to my self-image and the belief that my value is attached to certain socially constructed stages.

5. I will meet my goals and find my unique version of success at the time that's right for me.

34. "I'm unworthy"

I want to acknowledge that while all negative self-talk is harmful to some degree, there are definitely a few examples in this book that require much more time and attention to unlearn. Among the top three gnarliest things to believe about yourself is that you're unworthy.

When I say gnarly, I mean there is self-talk that we have been so strongly conditioned to believe that it can feel as real as our own heartbeat. When we tell ourselves that we are undeserving or unworthy, we are devaluing ourselves to the bottom of the barrel— many describe feeling like they're nothing or that they haven't done anything in life that makes them a worthwhile person.

It's a particularly tough chapter to infuse with levity because on its face, this *is* an incredibly painful thing to experience. Language like "unworthy" or "unlovable" can undermine a person's entire life, causing them to behave in ways that align with their self-description. It impacts the decisions we make, the people we allow into our lives, and the way we treat ourselves when we're struggling.

KNOWING OUR UNCONDITIONAL HUMAN WORTH

The possibility of being undeserving or unworthy is based on the "logic" that our existence and value are entirely conditional. The conditions may be those set by our parents, society, or relationships we're in. We learned that to be loved, we had to do something, be someone, or prove ourselves—worthiness was defined by something outside of ourselves.

One of my very favorite workbooks to suggest to clients, and I eagerly suggest it to you now, is *The Self-Esteem Workbook* written by Dr. Glenn R. Schiraldi. There is one page in particular that had an enormous impact on me and that I have adopted as a kind of code to live by. I have a printed copy of it accessible at any moment should my dog, Sunny, not be there to lick me for minutes on end in her unconditionally loving way. Yes—I am *that* dog mom.

Dr. Schiraldi shares these profound words: "'Unconditional human worth' means that you are important and valuable as a person because your essential, core self is unique and precious; of infinite, eternal, unchanging value; and good. Unconditional human worth implies that you are as precious as any other person" (Schiraldi 2016, 33).

I really believe that someone who *feels* undeserving is the *most* deserving of hearing the exact words that they need to learn to live by. Dr. Schiraldi goes on to list what he refers to as "Howard's Laws of Human Worth." I want to share with you a scribbled version of this wisdom and encourage you to take a photo or make a copy of the page—you can hang it up somewhere you can always read it, fold it into a tiny square and put it in your wallet, or print out copies and flier up the city you live in.

the basics of human worth

(HOWARD'S LAWS OF HUMAN WORTH)

1. all have infinate, internal, eternal, and unconditional worth as people

2. all have equal worth as people. worth is not comparative or competitive.

   ⇒ although you might be better at sports or academics, and I might be better at social skills,

   * we both have * equal worth * as human beings *

3. externals neither add nor diminish worth.

   e.g. money, looks, performance, achievements } these only increase one's market or social worth.

   worth as a person, however, is infinite and unchanging.

4. worth is stable and never in jeapordy! (even if someone rejects you)

5. worth doesn't have to be earned or proved. it already exists. just recognize, accept, and appreciate it.

credit: Glenn Schiraldi, *The Self-Esteem Workbook*

35. "Sure, but..."

Often when a client hears me say something they deeply resonate with, they reflect it back at me only to follow it with a "but...". When I hear the B word, I passionately describe how self-sabotaging it can be. Then I always make the same dad joke because it makes me laugh: "You are only allowed to have one but—and it's the one on your body."

When we use the word "but" after we state an empowered thought, it typically negates or minimizes the positive energy of the first clause. That first part is usually something we need to hear, some wisdom that we've learned to believe in, or something we'd like to do. Instead of letting it echo in our mental chamber, most of us feel compelled to disclaim, justify, or make an excuse. Here are some examples, some of which I'm sure will be familiar:

I want to go to the gym, but I can never seem to make it a habit.

I know that I deserve better, but I can't seem to date the right people.

I want to pursue my favorite hobby as a career, but I'm really scared.

I know I am not unworthy, but I can't stop thinking about being rejected.

REPLACE "BUT" WITH "AND"

In the case of negative self-talk, we can't afford to dismiss any moment of positivity or optimism. Luckily, there's a very simple approach: replace "but" with "and."

It may feel or sound a little strange saying this at first because it is not a typical sentence formation, but the slight shift in language communicates to our mind that two fairly opposite things can be true at the same time. It also has a neutralizing effect on the negative part of the sentence. Say the following phrases aloud and compare how the nuanced shift changes the energy of the sentence.

I'm open to trying *and* I'm afraid to fail.

I want to learn how to love my body *and* it's really hard work.

I know that I can do this on my own *and* it's difficult to picture it working out.

Using "and" helps us to stay empowered instead of unintentionally invalidating ourselves with "*but* it's hard," "*but* I'm scared," "*but* I'm so unmotivated."

SEARCH AND REPLACE

Write down five to ten of your own sentences that usually include "but" in the equation, just as I did above. Take a pen or marker and cross out the "but." Feel free to make it dramatic. Then, connect the clauses using "and"—read the new statements aloud. Finally, cross out the entire second part of the statement. Practice confidently saying the first part. Take a moment to revel in how much more inspiring and empowering it feels.

36. "I don't have any real talents or skills"

Well, I suppose you *could* learn how to juggle—or you'll just have to read this chapter and stop talking smack.

Every single human has talents and skills; our brain is far too complex and untapped to indulge in our inner critic's commentary. Sure, not everyone is Einstein or Oprah, but you'll just have to get over that. Neither you nor I can claim to have discovered gravity; it just is what it is.

Again, this is where we practice accepting that we might be considered quite ordinary as compared to all those humans who have done super world-changing things. Now, what we *don't* have is a crystal ball, so whether there are some world-changing vibes in our future, we simply don't know.

UNCOVER YOUR POTENTIAL

Whether you've been in an environment in which your instincts and interests were nurtured has a big impact on what potential gets tapped into. Here are some to-do items for you if you don't want to do the juggling thing:

- **Do a reality check.** Is it *really* true that you have no talents or skills or cool qualities? Write as extensive a list as you can.

- **Change the way you think about what constitutes a talent or a skill.** I'm dope at reading people, but every narcissist I've encountered didn't like that about me. Did their interpretation of it make it any less of a talent? Plus, what you may not consider a skill, someone else might.

- **Write down any accomplishments you've had using your objective mind.** If you taught your dog how to do a neat trick, write it down.

- **What do the people closest to you—who authentically know you—say about you?** What would your best friend or favorite family member include in your list of abilities?

- **Travel back in time and reflect on some of the things you loved to do as a child.** The uninhibited and open nature of our little selves will typically give us some interesting insight into our early interests and inclinations. Were you a Lego genius?

- **Remind yourself that it is never too late.** Do you want to learn a new skill or nurture a budding, untapped interest? All you need is the belief that it's perfectly okay to discover talents and acquire skills at any point in your life.

- **Reflect on why you tell yourself you don't have any skills or talents.** What has conditioned you to believe that? Is there something you loved but weren't given the chance to cultivate?

- **Choose:** You can accept being ordinary (if that's even the case), or you can live your life in a more fulfilled way by tapping into more of your potential and constantly learning new things.

37. "I need to be successful"

Our society has taught us to idealize success in any form and to devalue and dread the possibility of failure—or worse yet...being an average Joe. In our achievement-focused culture, there is an outrageous emphasis on successful outcomes, which quickly become synonymous with our worth as a human being.

My parents grew up in Russia and went to school on *Saturdays*—so, you better believe that if I didn't come home with that shiny report card, shimmering with A-pluses, it wasn't good enough. I remember once crumpling up my report card and stepping on it because I was so upset about my first B-plus. I remember pulling it out from the bottom of my bag and embarrassedly handing it over to my father, who was irritated at my attempt to make the subpar outcome disappear. He said something like, "What's going on with this B? You'll just have to work harder next time." I'm sure you have your own version of the story, whether it was your family, culture, or social norms that instilled in you a deep-seated fear of not living up to the expectations of success.

Imagine that two people—let's say Stu and Bert—are thinking about changing career paths because they aren't satisfied with their work. They would have to go back to school to do this. Which of the following sounds more like you?

Stu:

- *What if once I do it, I'm still not happy?*

- *At the end, I'll owe so much money.*

- *What if I can't hack doing what I want to do?*

- *What will people think if it doesn't work out?*

Bert:

- *It's exciting to think about taking on this new challenge.*

- *I missed learning in classes. I'll finally get to take ones I like.*

- *It's going to be challenging, but I know I'll be happier.*

- *I wonder if I can study abroad so that I can explore a new city while doing what I enjoy?*

Whose responses seem more familiar to you? Stu's fear-based thoughts have everything to do with the *outcome*. They are self-doubting and question trying this new endeavor. Bert's comments focus on what he can learn, grow from, or be excited about. He may have some worries, but his ultimate self-talk is full of curiosity and positivity, as well as focused on the *process*.

Who do you think will be more likely to attempt this new endeavor?

FOCUS ON THE PROCESS

When our self-worth is derived simply from knowing we put in the effort and were courageous enough to try something new, then the *process* itself is fulfilling on its own, regardless of whether we "succeed" or "fail." This allows us to live in a more present state of mind because we are not stuck in a constant state of future-thinking rooted in our fear of failing. We are much more interested in getting to authentically express ourselves and manifesting our dreams.

PRO TIP: Another way to look at this is from the perspective of a challenge versus threat mentality, which was looked at in the realm of sport psychology and athlete success (Fader 2016). We can choose to see an experience as a *threat*, hyperfocusing on all the things that could go wrong; or we can look at a situation as a *challenge* that we can take on and ultimately learn from.

FOCUS ON THE PROCESS

Write down three examples of things you'd like to succeed at. Then, write down corresponding statements—one statement that highlights your desire for the outcome, and one statement that shows your interest in the process.

Any time you want to try something new, write it down in big bold letters on a piece of paper. Immediately write down five things that you will likely learn from the experience. If you're already in the process of working toward a particular outcome, make a point to frequently and intentionally connect to the present moment by noting anything you're grateful for or learning during the experience.

38. "I feel like I'm broken"

I'm fucked-up. I've got too much baggage. Who would want someone like me around?

If you have ever said aloud or thought any version of that, please picture me swooping up your younger self into a tight bear hug. Often, we believe that we are broken because our body and mind carry a history of pain and trauma and it shows up in our interactions and life experiences. Many of us are adamant that there is something very wrong with us and exhaust ourselves trying to hide it from important people in our life because of our deep sense of shame. To identify ourselves as broken is to imply that the hardships we may have been through in life, no matter how little control we had over them at the time, somehow made us less than and unfixable.

What's worse is that this belief is strengthened not only by the way we talk to ourselves but also by how very little mindfulness and compassion are emphasized in Western culture. The longer I study humans, sadly, the more I notice how few of us know how to interact with each other in emotionally adaptive and mindful ways. It sucks, but they don't teach this shit in school.

Unfortunately, many people don't intentionally work on being more psychologically minded and self-aware. This lack of awareness ripples out in interpersonal interactions and can negatively affect people who are convinced they're damaged goods.

At best, humans suck at knowing what to say or ask when someone is suffering; at worst, there is a lack of empathy toward people who struggle with their mental health, which perpetuates stigmas that those of us who suffer beyond a baseline level of self-criticism (often those with a history of trauma, anxiety, depression, etc.) are fundamentally damaged in some way. I say all this to remind you that our perception of being broken is in large part a function of a culture that does not honor imperfection but devalues and demeans it.

ACCEPT YOURSELF AS HUMAN

If you are reading this chapter and you identify in any way with the feeling that something about you is not only broken but also unfixable, I want to take a moment to tell you how very, very untrue that is. You are a human who has experienced life, possibly in some pretty painful ways. There is no easy fix or sass or anecdote that I can share that will make you stop believing this about yourself in one fell swoop.

That being said, there *is* a simple choice that you can practice making every day: when you are feeling particularly bad about yourself in this way, instead of continuing to indulge the thought and the shame (which feed each other), try repeating any of the following statements. Next time your mind tells you that you're broken, choose to say:

I am a human who has suffered.

I am whole, even though I struggle.

I do not need fixing. I need healing.

Remember that the more you incorporate self-compassion into your self-talk and daily practice, the more you will slowly cease to see yourself as damaged in any way.

PRO TIP: If you want a more creative way to challenge yourself, learn about the Japanese art of Wabi-Sabi, which is premised on seeing the beauty in broken and imperfect things in all of life. To get creative, you can do some DIY kintsugi repair, which involves taking broken pottery and putting it back together by using gold powder (that's the authentic way) or metallic powder (just as great!). *Kintsugi* translates to mean "golden repair" (Kempton 2018). Not only is this a mindful way of observing how something broken can be made whole again, but it also allows us to give something that is indeed broken a new life—and ultimately marvel at the beauty of imperfection.

39. "I don't think my struggles are that big of a deal"

Well, if you really mean it, then I'm not sure there's more to say.

But just in case you're invalidating your suffering and minimizing your experience, I'll make this simple: if your struggles cause you pain or distress or affect your quality of life, then they're a big enough deal to pay attention to. Your struggles are unique and very real to you. Comparing experiences of suffering is simply not an option in my book because everyone's life circumstances are very different. If you're hurting, you deserve the same thoughtfulness and relief that you would want for someone else. Case closed!

40. "I'm not enough or I'm too much"

If we consistently engage in any of the first thirty-nine examples of harmful habits of mind and negative self-talk discussed in this book, we are destined to end up here. When meaningful people in our lives condition us to believe that there is something we don't have enough of or have too much of, they are teaching us that they have conditions we must meet to be acceptable or lovable. We grow up learning to look for clues in our interpersonal interactions that will confirm or deny whether we are in fact "not enough" or "too much" of something. That way, we can preemptively make sure that no one sees how flawed we (perceive) we are.

In closing out this book, I'd like to take a moment to be vulnerable about my own negative self-talk that cropped up even as I wrote confidently about ways to ditch it. With each round of edits, I worried about what readers would think about this book. Did I say the most important things about each self-talk example? What if little of this was compelling or too much of it redundant? Would you learn anything you didn't already know?

On the bright side—and that is ultimately where I would love for you to land—I did use as many of the tricks of the trade I shared with you. I noted the noisy critic with nonjudgment, normalized that it is scary to put myself out there, and ultimately used my values (self-growth and supporting the growth of others) to orient my behavior instead of my emotions (in this case, namely fear). I hope this book makes you feel less alone in taking on the genuine challenges of changing one of the most robust mental habits humans have, and more hopeful that you will be able to take that challenge on without judging your process along the way.

HEAL THE WOUNDS ONCE AND FOR ALL

Allow me to illuminate the preposterousness of the concept that we could ever measure our enoughness when the criteria were created by an unhealed human or *anyone* else that isn't the one living your life. Have you ever bought a bag of potato chips that you were craving, excitedly tore it open, and discovered that three-quarters of the bag was air? Do you recall that moment when you realized your craving wasn't at all satisfied, as you reached into the empty bag one last time, fingers covered in grease and crumbs? You crumpled up the bag in a huff—what a rip-off.

Let that be, once and for all, your only definition of what "not enough" looks like.

Let's imagine you have a mural in front of you where you can paint all of the shitty words and thoughts you've used against yourself. Take a step back and look at the wall for one last moment and acknowledge the harm that self-talk has inflicted on you. Then come back to the wall, and with heavy, painful strokes, cross out every one of those words. In the space next to each one, paint the new, healing words you plan to bring into your life. Take a step back and read those words aloud to yourself. Notice how it feels to hear yourself say these words.

And never look back.

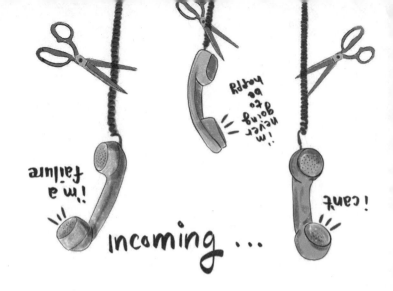

REFERENCES

Beck, Judith. 2020. *Cognitive Behavior Therapy: Basics and Beyond*. 3rd ed. New York: Guilford Press.

Brach, Tara. 2004. *Radical Acceptance: Embracing Your Life With the Heart of a Buddha*. New York: Bantam Dell.

Brown, Brené. 2007. *I Thought It Was Just Me (But It Isn't): Making the Journey from "What Will People Think?" to "I Am Enough."* New York: Penguin Random House.

Brown, Brené. 2010. *The Gifts of Imperfection: Let Go of Who You Think You're Supposed to Be and Embrace Who You Are*. Center City, MN: Hazelden.

Cacioppo, John, Stephanie Cacioppo, and Jackie Gollan. "The Negativity Bias: Conceptualization, Quantification, and Individual Differences." *Behavioral and Brain Sciences* 37(3): 309–310.

Chödrön, Pema. 2000. *When Things Fall Apart: Heart Advice for Hard Times*. Boston: Penguin Books.

Chödrön, Pema. 2015. *Fail, Fail Again, Fail Better: Wise Advice for Leaning into the Unknown*. Louisville, CO: Sounds True.

Deschene, Lori. 2021. "How to Deal with Unfairness and Change the Things You Can." *Tiny Buddha: Simple Wisdom for Complex Lives* (blog). August 4. https://tinybuddha.com

/blog/how-to-deal-with-unfairness-and-change-the-things
-you-can/.

Doidge, Norman. 2007. *The Brain That Changes Itself.*
New York: Penguin Books.

Dweck, Carol S. 2007. *Mindset: The New Psychology of Success.*
New York: Ballantine Books.

Fader, Jonathan. 2016. *Life as Sport: What Top Athletes Can
Teach You About How to Win in Life.* Boston: DaCapo Press.

Germer, Christopher K. 2009. *The Mindful Path to Self-
Compassion: Freeing Yourself from Destructive Thoughts
and Emotions.* New York: Guilford Press.

Germer, Christopher, and Kristin Neff. 2019. "Mindful
Self-Compassion (MSC)." In *Handbook of Mindfulness-Based
Programmes: Mindfulness Interventions from Education to
Health and Therapy,* edited by Itai Itvzan. London:
Routledge.

Kabat-Zinn, Jon. 2005. *Wherever You Go, There You Are:
Mindfulness Meditation in Everyday Life.* New York:
Hyperion.

Kempton, Beth. 2018. *Wabi Sabi: Japanese Wisdom for a
Perfectly Imperfect Life.* New York: Harper Design.

Krimer, Katie. 2020. *The Essential Self-Compassion Workbook
for Teens: Overcome Your Inner Critic and Fully Embrace
Yourself.* Emeryville, CA: Rockridge Press.

Lethbridge, Jessica, Hunna Watson, Sarah Egan, Helen Street,
and Paula Nathan. 2011. "The Role of Perfectionism,

Dichotomous Thinking, Shape and Weight Overevaluation, and Conditional Goal Setting in Eating Disorders." *Eating Behaviors* 12(3): 200–206.

Lewis, Michael. 1998. "Emotional Competence and Development." In *Improving Competence Across the Lifespan*, edited by Dolores Pushkar, William M. Bukowski, Alex E. Schwartzman, Dale M. Stack, and Donna R. White. New York: Plenum Press.

Luby, Joan, Andy Belden, Jill Sullivan, Robin Hayen, Amber McCadney, and Ed Spitznagel. 2009. "Shame and Guilt in Preschool Depression: Evidence for Elevations in Self-Conscious Emotions in Depression as Early as Age 3." *Journal of Child Psychology and Psychiatry, and Allied Disciplines* 50(9): 1156–1166.

Mantini, Dante, and Wim Vanduffel. 2013. "Emerging Roles of the Brain's Default Network." *The Neuroscientist: A Review Journal Bringing Neurobiology, Neurology, and Psychiatry* 19(1): 76–87.

Merriam-Webster, s.v. "Self-Talk (n.)," accessed February 15, 2021, https://www.merriam-webster.com/dictionary/self-talk.

Merriam-Webster, s.v. "Thought (n.)," accessed January 12, 2021, https://www.merriam-webster.com/dictionary/thought.

Neff, Kristin. 2011. *Self-Compassion: The Proven Power of Being Kind to Yourself*. New York: HarperCollins.

Neff, Kristin, and Christopher Germer. 2018. *The Mindful Self-Compassion Workbook: A Proven Way to Accept Yourself, Build Inner Strength, and Thrive*. New York: Guilford Press.

Nhat Hanh, Thich. 1995. "Interbeing with Thich Nhat Hanh: An Interview." *Tricycle*, Summer 1995, https://tricycle.org/magazine/interbeing-thich-nhat-hanh-interview/.

Salzberg, Sharon. 2002. *Lovingkindness: The Revolutionary Art of Happiness*. Boston: Shambhala Publications.

Schiraldi, Glenn R. 2016. *The Self-Esteem Workbook*. 2nd ed. Oakland, CA: New Harbinger Publications.

Tolle, Eckhart. 2004. *The Power of Now: A Guide to Spiritual Enlightenment*. Novato, CA: New World Library.

Woods, Rachel F. 2018. "How to Stop Black-and-White Thinking," May 31, PsychCentral, https://psychcentral.com/blog/cultivating-contentment/2018/05/how-to-stop-black-and-white-thinking#3.

KATIE KRIMER, LCSW, is a psychotherapist at a thriving practice in New York, NY; and founder and coach at a wellness/growth coaching company called Growspace. She immigrated from Russia at a young age, and grew up in New Jersey. She received her BS and MA degrees in clinical psychology from the University of Washington and Boston University respectively, and earned her clinical social work degree and LCSW license from NYU. She has earned a certificate in mindfulness and psychotherapy from the renowned Institute for Meditation and Psychotherapy, and will pursue a two-year mindfulness meditation teacher certification under the mentorship of Tara Brach and Jack Kornfield. She is author of *The Essential Self-Compassion Workbook for Teens,* and is deeply passionate about helping others develop a more authentic and vulnerable way of living, supporting humans through life struggles, and teaching the practice of mindfulness and self-compassion.

MORE BOOKS from
NEW HARBINGER PUBLICATIONS

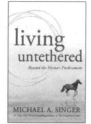

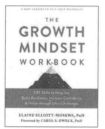

Real change *is* possible

For more than forty-five years, New Harbinger has published proven-effective self-help books and pioneering workbooks to help readers of all ages and backgrounds improve mental health and well-being, and achieve lasting personal growth. In addition, our spirituality books offer profound guidance for deepening awareness and cultivating healing, self-discovery, and fulfillment.

Founded by psychologist Matthew McKay and Patrick Fanning, New Harbinger is proud to be an independent, employee-owned company. Our books reflect our core values of integrity, innovation, commitment, sustainability, compassion, and trust. Written by leaders in the field and recommended by therapists worldwide, New Harbinger books are practical, accessible, and provide real tools for real change.

newharbingerpublications